33 miles
from Washington

33 miles

from Washington

Book: One

TD McRoy

Library of Congress Control Number: 2017952983

ISBN Paperback: 978-0-9989966-9-1
ISBN eBook: 978-1-947368-25-5

Cover Design: Troy McRoy
Interior Design: Ghislain Viau

To Helen M. Ambrose, someone who was there during life's lows and surely wound the clock that led to life's current highs. Thank you for uplifting me.

CONTENTS

ACKNOWLEDGEMENTS

I WOULD LIKE TO EXPRESS MY SINCERE AND DEEPEST appreciation to my parents, especially my mom for encouraging and supporting me throughout the research. I would like to express my gratitude to Bernie Collins & Steve Hobbs, true friends and longtime mentors for allowing me to always be me.

I am grateful for all they did to shape me at the start of my career. It was those early years of teaching that still strongly guide my efforts.

This book, *33 Miles from Washington,* is a showcase of quantum spirit energy that was captured on film on October 22, 2005. The images held within these pages can be considered otherworldly. As impressive as the discovered images are, what's more impressive are the number of famous historical figures that were captured at one location. For that reason, we set out to find a logical explanation for this phenomenon.

We were not prepared for what we discovered. In part, we discovered a treasure trove of unclaimed historical information that catalogs how the Ark of the Covenant was seized and then transported from the Temple of Solomon.

The evidence we uncovered tells of an ancient journey from the sands of Jerusalem to the rocky shores of New Jersey, where the Ark of the Covenant initially landed upon American soil.

We were able to reverse-engineer details that led back to a lonely log cabin in the woods, just some 33 miles from the center of Washington, D.C.

It would be there where I encountered some of the greatest leaders the world had to offer. And it would appear that in those men—those chosen men—they would act as protectors to guard the final resting place of the Ark of the Covenant. Although my claims are truly fantastic, the information that is shared in this book shall act as only the launchpad to a potential scientific breakthrough in quantum mechanics. Since the completion of this book in 2012, members of my research organization, CPI Investigations, and I have made great advancements in research. However, we decided to use this work as a first semester textbook to our new members. For that reason, we only touch upon our later creations like the "Iroquois Technology", which allows us to discover quantum energy from nearly any type of video or film footage. We are hoping that once you have finished this book, you will be compelled to join our world-wide open-source research project. To date we have discovered more than three hundred and fifty quantum spirits on film. All those images will be available to CPI members (only) who join our open-source research project at https://www.comusparanormalinvestigations.org/.

What you are about to read in this book was the start of that effort. Please keep an open mind and we look forward to working with you as a CPI investigator; so please enjoy.

ABOUT THE AUTHOR

Td McRoy (born February 23, 1965) is an American physicist, and fourth dimensional theorist. He has been an instructor and is the current Chief Executive Director for CPI investigations, an independent research group of physicists that seeks to prove a fourth dimension exists within the known third dimensional space. He is also the creator of the Paranormal Activity Open-source Research Project. The theory of the human soul and transitional "neutrinos" is based on his "Subatomic googolplex singularity" theory.

McRoy coined the term QEIN: Quantum Energy In Nature. The term is used to describe the quantum figures that his research organization publicly displays.

Born: February 23, 1965 (age 52)

Montgomery County Maryland, U.S.

Residence: United States

Nationality: American

Fields of research: Physics

Organization: Chief Executive Director, CPI Investigations

Known for: *Dimension 4 Research*
             Midatomic Realm Theory
             Subatomic Googolplex Singularity Theory
             The QEIN Theory
             The Three Stage Tornado Model Theory

McRoy is the developer and creator of "Iroquois Technology," a complex program that helps to display polyhedra in dimension four. He has become known to a wider audience through his earlier books. More recently, he's becoming known for his research into the midatomic realm & studies in dimension Four.

Author TD McRoy has spent over eleven years researching the possibility that the Ark of the Covenant is housed in Comus, Maryland. He is encouraged that the evidence that led him to uncover this cataclysmic revelation is sure to expand interest in George Washington as more than just an inspirational leader. Mr. McRoy provides more than just a theory to readers; he provides one hundred and forty pages of colorful evidence discovered at the Comus log cabin that supports what he believes is the current location of the Ark of the Covenant.

WARNING: TRESPASSING

Any current and future members of CPI are requested not to commit the following acts at the Comus, Maryland, property where the photographs in this book were taken: photographing, capturing, or removing from the Comus or any other property where CPI is known to investigate. CPI leadership considers any and all of these acts as a violation of our Criminal Trespassing Guidelines.

In most cases, criminal trespassing is defined as entering or remaining on a premises or property without the authorization, license, or privilege to do so. Usually, notice against entering or remaining can either be delivered in oral or written fashion by the property owner or an authorized agent. That is state law: CPI has chosen to use this same law to assure no members of CPI Investigation violate that law.

Trespassing consequences are generally misdemeanor or a felony in some cases. That is what the law recommends, we at CPI cannot enforce that law. However, we will immediately drop anyone from our membership rolls who have violated our criminal trespassing guidelines. Anyone applying for membership who violates these guidelines will be excluded from membership indefinitely.

DISCLAIMER
Graphic Content, Spiritual Powers, and Scientific Inquiry

Due to the graphic nature of the photographs in this book, reader discretion is advised. Because of its findings, CPI believes that mortal man is never to look upon the powers that the ark might possess unless "Thee" is considered holy by the Lord, so pursuit is not recommended: do so at your own risk.

In addition, CPI is not sanctioned by any scientific body or community. We operate on our own terms, and though we are wholly dedicated to uncovering the truth to mortal existence, we plan to remain a volunteer group of researchers and scientists dedicated to studying scientific advancement in the field of quantum mechanics and paranormal studies, as we are convinced they are all one in the same.

RESEARCH METHODS AND A
NOTE ABOUT PHOTOGRAPHS

THIS BOOK ATTEMPTS TO DEMONSTRATE WITH visual proof the existence of quantum energy in nature by use of cinematic evidence. In addition, we focus on the theory that most supernatural events that occur in nature are all related and have only one culprit.

More than three dozen captured images of quantum energy have been selected for this publication, though CPI has studied over 350 in the past decade of research. The samples were cropped directly from recorded video evidence.

In addition, some of the photos throughout the book have been color inverted to show hidden pockets of quantum energy that are not visible to the naked eye. Other images have been color enhanced to make seeing the spirits easier, and are noted as such throughout. No other alterations have been made to the images.

INVITATION

THIRTY-THREE MILES FROM WASHINGTON IS BASED on never-before-revealed evidence discovered at an abandoned log cabin in Comus, Maryland on October 22, 2005. This vision of history involves the father of America, George Washington, by chronicling how the Ark of the Covenant was obtained by King George the Second and hidden in Maryland farm country thirty-three miles outside of Washington D.C.

The book includes proof that will strongly support the final resting place of the Ark of the Covenant, as well as a supernatural theory that George Washington should be considered more of a deity than a man.

The first president of the United States of America carried a world secret to his grave that's only now been uncovered. This book focuses on the secret deeds of George Washington rather than duplicate information previously covered by well-known authors like Joseph Ellis, Ron Chernow, James Flexner, David McCullough, and Washington Irving.

I am thrilled to take this opportunity to provide proof that such an event took place. I believe that the world will never fully accept the evidence of what happened in this lonely stretch of rural America between me and the spiritual realm. I am at peace with those who feel my claims to be false as my initial response to these naysayers is ambivalence. I also hope readers will share their thoughts and stories with the CPI community at https://www.comusparanormalin-vestigations.org/.

Chapter 1

SUMMARY OF EVENTS LEADING TO THE REMOVAL OF THE ARK OF THE COVENANT

THE LAST KNOWN LOCATION OF THE LOST ARK OF the Covenant was in the temple of Solomon prior to the siege of Jerusalem. The Ark is one of the Bible's holiest objects and was reported to be covered with pure gold. It was a wooden box that contained the Ten Commandments. Many scholars from around the world debate the actual location of the Ark. Some believe it's under the Sphinx, in France, or possibly near London's Temple tube station. Others believe it remains in Jerusalem beneath the Temple Mount.

However, Orlando-based supernatural society Comus Paranormal Investigations (CPI) believes to have accidently stumbled upon information that was never meant to be revealed to the public. CPI's recent research contradicts earlier claims of the Ark of the Covenant's location.

As CPI's executive director, I discovered a rare supernatural photograph that was taken on October 22, 2005 in Comus, Maryland, suggesting that possibly this could be the final resting place for the Ark of the Covenant. Before the three original photographs could be determined as authentic, our group took a fresh look at the legends behind the Ark of the Covenant and, we believe, disproved other theories in the process.

The only way CPI could prove what the images suggested was to re-examine the story of the Ark of the Covenant. With the 2005 photographs in hand, the group decided to work backwards, starting with the photograph and tracing the steps back to Jerusalem, in the year 587 BC, where a second siege was being led by the King of Babylon, Nebuchadnezzar II. King Nebuchadnezzar, as part of the secret society the Freemason, entered Jerusalem with his army, and the Ark was still believed to be in Solomon's Temple.

Meanwhile, Jeremiah had been imprisoned by the Judean King Zedekiah, while Nebuchadnezzar troops arrived to slaughter all the sons of Zedekiah. Nebuchadnezzar recognized Jeremiah as a member of the Freemason society, and ordered his imperial guards to "Take him and look after him; don't harm him but do for him whatever he asks."

Some skeptics believe that King Nebuchadnezzar's troops destroyed the Ark along with the Temple of Solomon during that siege. CPI believes this is untrue: The Ark was built at the command of God, in accord with the prophetic vision Moses experienced on Mount Sinai. As such, no man could destroy God's holy creation. As Freemasons, Nebuchadnezzar and Jeremiah believed they were tasked with keeping the Ark safe.

The true reason for the siege of Jerusalem was a deliberate display concocted by the Knights Templar and the Freemasons to divert Zedekiah's soldiers away from the Ark of the covenant. The devastating slaughter waged outside of the temple walls was a way to weaken any of the Ark's protectors. Most historians believe that Jeremiah was released by the Babylonians and hid in a watch-tower in the city of Benjamin eight miles from Jerusalem.

We discovered information that shows Jeremiah traveled to Ireland after being released, and he was granted Zedekiah's daughter by King Nebuchadnezzar to accompany him. He brought gold and stone tablets to the Freemasons of Ireland that came directly from the siege at Jerusalem, which continued to rage. King Nebuchadnezzar and the Knights Templar priests were considered warriors of God and removed the Ark from the temple of Solomon and relocated it 2388 miles away, in India, where it would remain for decades.

Soon, all the original conspirators passed away. In the 1750s, word about a mysterious artifact in India reached King George II of Great Britain. As a Freemason, he confided in a good friend named Doctor Sir Hans Sloane. Sloane had been the President of the College of Physicians and succeeded Sir Isaac Newton as President of the Royal Society.

One artifact in Sloane's 71,000-piece collection that impressed the King was a small tablet that provided proof of a siege that occurred in Jerusalem around 597 B.C. Sloane refused to part with this piece. On January 11, 1753, at the age of 92, Sloane passed away, and he bequeathed his entire collection of antiques to Parliament in exchange for a payment of £20,000 to his heirs. After the death of Sloane, Parliament established the British Museum to house his collection. King George had since passed away, but once Parliament got their hands on Sloane's ancient artifacts, it would take them another three years before being able to trace many of the items back to the siege at Jerusalem by way of Ireland where many were delivered by Jeremiah. Figuring that information found in the Old Testament was factual, Parliament concluded that it was possible to locate and capture the Ark of the Covenant.

In 1786, General Cornwallis was sent to India to safeguard further research into locating the Ark of the Covenant. In this same year, Cornwallis was knighted, then appointed as Governor General and commander-in-chief of India.

Meanwhile, Freemason George Washington was elected first President of the United States of America.

During this time, Cornwallis became engaged in the Third Anglo-Mysore War in India. Meanwhile, the Ark of the Covenant was moved to Ethiopia in an attempt to hide it. While crossing the Arabian Sea, Cornwallis's troops intercepted the Ark. Contemporary documents revealed that whenever the ark was in transit, it was carefully wrapped in an animal skin veil, covered with a blue cloth which made it quite easy to spot for anyone granted with this information.

The Knights Templar priests were the only mortals granted permission by God to make physical contact with the Ark of the Covenant. Once word reached Great Britain that the Ark was under British rule, members of Parliament secretly ordered the Ark sent far away to a land where the world would never consider its location as feasible. Fearing discovery of the Ark, Parliament secretly ordered it be moved to America. There, Ark would be entrusted to President George Washington and the Freemason society.

Upon secret orders from the Grand Lodge of England, architect Peter Charles L'Enfant was to not only prepare the new capital city for the coming of the Ark, but to spread vicious rumors and Satanic symbols to quell any potential talk about the Ark of the Covenant being in America. These masterminds of deception knew that no one would ever consider looking for a holy symbol of God masked in and surrounded in the symbols of the occult and Lucifer. For those who wished to praise the images seen in the masonic Washington laid symbols, death by human sacrifice was an ideal way to eliminate those who got too close to the truth.

We finalized our research when we learned that the final resting place for the Ark of the Covenant was part of a riddle based on the number 33. George Washington was born on February 22, 1732, but by the British calendar he was born on February 11, 1732. Combined, those dates make up the number 33. George Washington had 33 revolutionary Freemason generals, and other than the Knights Templar, no others were allowed to attend the ceremony to bury the Ark.

The location where CPI believes the Ark now rests is exactly 33 miles from the center of Washington, D.C. Traveling outward from the monuments brings visitors to a log cabin set close to the edge of a two-lane country road.

Many might wonder how it would be physically possible for such a divine device to remain hidden under a simple log cabin since the late 1700s without being accidentally discovered. The 2005 photographs show paranormal specters protecting the Ark, as well as other spirits granted the grand of grandeur's distinction of protecting the Ark from interlopers.

I interviewed a married couple who operate a country fruit stand three miles from where this cabin exists. This couple discussed several instances of paranormal activity in that area over the past 40 years. Although the married couple is unaware of the log cabin's potential biblical significance, they claim that every twenty years or so a total stranger will tell them that he or she was run off the property by a powerful force.

The photographs throughout this book support those claims of paranormal activity. Some of the photographs reveal images of generals of the American Revolutionary War. Since the photographs were taken on October 22, 2005, CPI concludes that these spirits have been given the honor to act as protector of the Ark based solely on the power that the Ark possesses.

If all of this can be proven based on images discovered on October 22, 2005, CPI members wonder why it's taken the scientific community so long to get here, which brings to mind the line from the motion picture *Raiders of the lost Ark*: "They're digging in the wrong place." Once our research was complete, the only other thing we needed to consider was how best to share our finding with the world. We agreed to tell this portion in story format exactly as it occurred on October 22, 2005. We hope you enjoy it.

Please keep an open mind about what you're about to discover.

Chapter 2

COMUS, MARYLAND

IT WAS ONE OF THOSE RARE, UNUSUALLY MILD, sun-filled days in a small northeastern town near Frederick, Maryland. It was October 22, 2005. I traveled far west of Washington, D.C., toward the sprawling hills to capture the essence of nature.

My gear consisted of a 5-megapixel camera to document the area's unique beauty, cultural heritage, and iconic history. As I traveled along the two-lane country road, the stunning views and cultural wonders of a time long past were evident all around me. I was excited to explore scenic vistas on such a clear, breathtaking, bright, sunny day.

After a while, I came upon an old, abandoned log cabin, which piqued my curiosity.

Although the cabin was rustic, possibly early colonial, it was the array of multi- color leaves in the trees and covering the property that captured my imagination. As a child, I grew up in a community called "Woodmoor" in suburban Maryland. In the front yard of my boyhood home were two very large oak trees, the memory of which compelled me to photograph thousands of stunning leaves covering the log cabin property.

Unlike during my childhood when I had to rake the leaves, I could enjoy these leaves. The landscaping duties chores assigned to me and my brother growing up, and for a moment the tender scene brought me warm serenity.

The day was mild and sunny, and there was hardly a breeze. I snapped three photographs of the aging cabin and the beautiful leaves. I noticed many species of trees changing color: red, green, purple, yellow, bronze, and olive. As a child, I was never able to appreciate the beauty of nature while performing my chores of raking, bagging, and compiling leaves. We never missed leaf collection day.

The first shot I took that October day occurred while I stood just at the outer perimeter of the property line, nearly in the middle of the deserted, two-lane country road. I stood quietly, camera in hand. I thought I'd heard several heavy footsteps moving slowly through the trees. These phantom steps seemed to keep perfect pace with the sound of twigs lightly snapping high above the log cabin, as if someone was clearing them to one side.

Though I saw nothing, I started to feel uncomfortable. Then, I heard what sounded like a small congregation of voices coming from the rear of the log cabin. The more I turned and pointed my ear in the direction of the voices, the softer the conversation seemed to become, not allowing me to zero in on any conversation.

Feeling chilled, I was ready to cut my photography session short. I quickly snapped the second photo. As I took this photograph, I stood only a few yards away from where I parked my car, just inside the split-rail fencing that stretched along the front of the property. Positive that I was completely alone, I still felt uneasy as total silence seemed to fall across the land.

No wind, no birds, nothing could be heard coming from the woods. It was as if there was an invisible veil of energy blocking out all sound. Though I was disturbed, I was not willing to depart with only two candid shots, so I pushed on, passing the front entranceway of the cabin door to take my third photograph of the day.

Suddenly, I was encapsulated with the feeling of being crowded by a horde of people, but nobody was there. I decided to slowly and deliberately make my way back toward my car. I paused for a moment and prepared to take another photograph, but that shot never happened.

As I attempted to focus the camera lens on the left side of the log cabin, I thought I saw a faint white flash move across the tiny LCD screen fitted to the backside of my camera. Almost immediately, an indescribable feeling washed over me. I turned quickly, abandoning my desire to take a fourth shot. It was at this moment that I felt something that could only be described as a large column of energy starting to rush from behind me.

Every tiny hair on the back of my neck stood erect and a cold chill ran down my spine. I could sense a massive block of energy rapidly approaching. I sensed gigantic charging footsteps coming up from behind me, so intense that they shook the ground beneath my feet. This caused the large maple leaves that I admired moments earlier to be hurled upward in my direction, forming a tidal wave of vegetation up and over my head as it was clear these large footsteps were responsible.

I had no time to react. There was no time for me to escape the phenomenon, so I pulled my shoulders in towards my chest and braced for an impact that knocked the air from my lungs.

I am not 100 percent sure if it was the impact that caused the evacuation of air from my lungs, or if it was the sheer horror of being attacked by something unseen.

Later, I described to a close friend that the rushing column of energy that moved toward me that morning felt as if I was about to be struck by a commuter train barreling down at top speed. Though the initial impact hit me square in the back, lifting me off my feet, I survived to share the story.

Just after the impact, I thought that maybe a hunter ran from the wooded area and somehow gotten close enough to shove me before I could see him or her.

I was initially upset at the thought of some hunter charging at me. Quickly, I became furious, picking myself up off the ground to confront the hunter. Facing the log cabin, I scanned the open area and did not see anyone. I assumed that whomever had assaulted me was now playing a game and must have ran out of view and was probably hiding behind me.

I pivoted on my left heel, searching for the culprit who had committed the assault, now facing the direction of my car that was still parked across the street in an area where a house once stood. The cold sweat of reality was about to hit me head-on. Spinning around once more looking for anyone or anything that had violently shoved me, I was out of explanations.

Now, facing the log cabin, I was met with a powerful thud located directly in front of where I stood. The sound was loud, deep and colossal—a warning not to take another step forward. As the earth rumbled, the anterior portion of my body was met with an invisible energy that extended from the top frontal portion of my head to below my kneecaps, only inches away from my face.

It felt like a thousand tiny finger-tips lightly touching me. Although I never saw anything standing before me, I felt compelled to tilt my chin upward as if I was dealing with something at least seven to eight feet tall. Whatever this was, it was now standing centimeters away from my face. That was when I concluded that whatever was standing in front of me could be supernatural.

I felt the static charge that the entity was giving off, keeping me at bay. With my heart pounding, I feared my heart might give out—I could feel my heartbeat in the axis of my throat.

This aerial view at right shows the exact location where each snapshot was taken (in yellow) as well as where the attack began (in red).

I calmly said these exact words in a very shaky barely audible voice. "Look," speaking to whatever was standing in front of me. "You do not need to scare me anymore; my car is right over there!" Pointing out my vehicle, I added, "I'm leaving." As soon as I said those words, I felt the energy that had been pressing up against me back away.

Slowly turning away, I calmly made my way across the two-lane road and back to my car.

When I reached the car, I opened the driver side door and glanced back across the property. I saw nothing out of the ordinary. All was calm. As I placed the seatbelt across

Aerial view of the Comus property

my chest, I noticed that my heart was pounding so fiercely that it caused the material on my favorite red Jeff Gordon racing jacket to pulsate.

My skin was cold, clammy, and shaky. I drove a few miles down the road, checking my rearview mirror frequently. I came upon a cider stand at the first intersection. I pulled over and parked. I took a deep breath then turned the ignition off. I stepped from my vehicle and walked over to where a man and woman were working. With legs seeming as if they were filled with Jell-O, I said in a weedy voice, "Hi, can I ask you a question?"

"Sure," the man and woman said, believing I was probably in desperate need of directions. I asked the couple how long they had been in the area. The man said he had lived in the area his entire life and his wife had been in the area since they had been married over thirty years earlier. I told the man and his wife the story that was still fresh in my mind as my heart rate returned to a more normal rhythm.

The man said he believed me because he had heard similar stories from others who had the same type of encounter in virtually the same location decades earlier. The man added that it had been at least 20 years since hearing a story like that, but nevertheless he believed my encounter whole-heartedly. He added that the only difference between my encounter and the other stories was that the other people had seen their attackers.

He said in those instances, the assailants were apparitions of Native Americans. I told the man and his wife I never saw whatever had attacked me, but I was positive that I had experienced their energy. It was at this moment that the lady suggested that it probably had something to do with the bright red Jeff Gordon racing jacket I had on.

Initially, I was not sure if the lady was attempting to make light of the situation by suggesting that not only race fans of NASCAR dislike Jeff Gordon and his 2001 winning ways, but most possibly Native American apparitions do so as well. I chuckled in response to her joke.

"Yeah, I guess Jeff Gordon has many haters," I said. Being dead serious, the woman corrected herself said, "No, that's not what I meant. I mean your Jeff Gordon racing jacket looks like the British Redcoat military jacket worn during the American Revolutionary War!

I bet you that's why they attacked you! They wanted you off their land!" Dismayed, I thanked the couple for sharing their knowledge of the area and headed back to my car.

"Marvelous!" I thought to myself sarcastically. I had stopped at the cider stand hoping to find anyone who could logically explain what had occurred at the log cabin and heard something else entirely.

At that moment, I did not believe ghosts existed. However, the casual encounter at the cider stand did nothing to ease my doubts. Just before I pulled away, the wife ran over to the passenger side of my car and said through the open window, "I bet you will find something in your photographs." That was the only time I ever saw or spoke with that couple.

It would be some time until I returned to that spot. I meandered around in an emotional hazy-funk for the rest of the day, trying to come to grips with what may or may not have occurred to me in those woods. By the end of the day, I was certain that I may have had some sort of physical episode, yet I had never had a stroke, seizure or other medical condition.

However, I felt that history meant little. New medical conditions can crop up anytime and anywhere. It would not be until the next morning that I would sit down and upload the images from the log cabin. I made it through the night and physically felt 100 percent better.

The next morning, I uploaded the three images from the previous day onto my home computer and studied the snapshots in the exact order that they were uploaded. By the time I reached the final photograph, nothing out of the ordinary was discovered. Completely relieved and satisfied by what I saw—or in this case, what I did not see in the photographs—I felt that I could start searching for a biological reason for the phenomenon.

The thought of having a medical illness was more acceptable to me than if I had been attacked by something otherworldly. I was not a paranormal investigator then, and knew very little about the field of study, and did not want any part of it. However, there still was an uneasy feeling that something non-medical occurred to me in Comus.

Twenty-four hours after the incident, I decided to take another look at the photographs. I noticed something that I missed the first time. Toward the right side of the first photo was a white spot. In my haste to enlarge the image, I clicked the mouse four times, causing the image of the white spot to fill my computer monitor.

The image was so disturbing that it made my eyes water. I quickly stood up and walked behind the chair as if the chair could somehow protect me from the ghostly image glaring from the screen. I could only stare at the image. Then I began to pace in a circle, holding the back of my head with one hand, refusing to believe what I saw.

At this point, there was no further reason to consider what had occurred in the woods was medical. The disturbing truth was staring me right in the face. From the image angle, it was difficult for me to tell if the entity was wearing some sort of mask, or if it was the actual face of a creature. Regardless, the being looked as if it has neither a mouth nor nose. The entity's right-side ear looked a bit lower than is usually reported in human-like apparitional sightings.

If this was not a spirit wearing some type of Indian war mask, the oddities in relation to this spirit leads me to assume that this creature possibly never walked Earth in a human form, or did so prior to recorded history of mankind. My first concern was that if such "quantum spirits" exist, are they controlled by boundaries? And if not, could they possibly travel great distances?

Basically, I was concerned that retaliation could be possible for me filming them. It's rumored that Native Americans never wanted their images captured on film, having something to do with their images being trapped within the image. Until I discovered the image of what I now call "The Comus Creature," I felt that all this was complete hogwash.

In light of what was staring back at me from the computer monitor, those stories now seemed possible. Some people might think it's exciting to capture proof of life after death.

Knowing that a spirit attacked me and later discovering that I'd captured the specter on film was not an exciting prospect. The entire incident became too surreal to deal with. What this meant to me was that theoretically I could be attacked by these same spirits anytime and at any location. Being pulled from my bed in the middle of the night by what was staring at me from the computer screen didn't sit well with me.

And at that very moment, I knew that life would never be the same for me again. I was not the type of person that generally use profanity but, I found myself blurting out the F-word as my mind continued to create more outrageous nightmarish scenarios.

To get confirmation on the images, I sent the photographs to two of my friends by e-mail. It wasn't long before both confirmed seeing the image of "The Comus Creature" within my snapshot. Realizing now that I could no longer deny what was evident in the photograph. I found myself cursing again; it was the only way I could truly describe my crumbling emotional state-of-mind.

That was Sunday, October 23, 2005.

It would be a while before I felt comfortable enough to view the photographs again in a constructive manner without fear. Once I discovered the image of what looked to be men and women from the Civil War era, I felt that the photographs could offer "mankind" a new perspective on existence. I had taken physics previously in school and felt that my best chance for determining this type of phenomenon would be in that field. I would relocate to Orlando, Florida, and begin a secret journey to continue my education to seek out the answers.

Chapter 3

THE DYALTOV PASS MYSTERY

IN 1959, TEN CROSS-COUNTRY SKIERS SET OFF ON A camping trip in Russia's Ural Mountains. Nine skiers died mysteriously, and the case remains unresolved.

Evidence shows that the nine hurriedly left their tents after cutting their way out with the use of sharp objects as if someone or something was blocking the tent's exit. Skis, food, and clothes were left behind as they ran into the woods in minus 30-degree temperatures. No animal or human tracks were ever discovered around the snowy tents. Investigators reported only the tracks of the nine skiers in the snow exiting the campgrounds.

Several of the members found dead appeared to have sustained injuries often seen in victims struck by trains.

The Skier before the Encounter

Recalling my own non-lethal experience, the encounters seem similar. Investigators concluded that the group died because of "a compelling unknown force." I believe that on October 22, 2005, I was attacked by a powerful unseen force in the woods.

Unlike the skiers, I survived my otherworldly ordeal and obtained photographic evidence to support my claim. I believe both incidents are related to supernatural phenomena.

The common denominator is that both incidents occurred in nature. What ultimately made my outcome different from the skiers was that my salvation was only thirty yards from where the incident occurred. I walked into the middle of these deities, whereas the skiers set up camp. With my

24

vehicle within proximity of where the attack took place, I feel that if I had been deeper into the woods that morning I might have died like those skiers.

The images that support CPI's theory show that quantum energy of Native American spirits protects the sacred land at Comus. It's possible that the quantum energy from the Ural Mountains and the Comus location might have more than just similarities, which we'll discuss at length later in the book.

I believe there are two figures seen in the photographs that are possibly connected with the Mansi People, an ancient tribes that inhabited the western Ural Mountains where the Russian skiers perished. Two captured images of quantum spirit energy may be direct decedents of the Mansi People, thereby connecting the Comus incident with The Dyatlov Pass Mystery.

It's my belief that whatever these "things" are, they can occupy small plots of land that can support thousands even possibly millions of quantum energy particles. I do feel that the odds of making camp or stumbling upon them in nature are nearly impossible, which is why so little evidence like this ever is captured—I was in the "right" place at the "wrong" time. Imagine how many people have probably captured what is seen in these photographs, but never take a second look. I only did was because I was confident I did not have a seizure or a stroke. So, I believed that there had to be something in the photographs to explain what happened.

My team and I assume many of these unidentified spirits never had human form.

The photograph below is the first of the three photographs that I took that day back in 2005. See this image and any of the photographs that appear in this book at https://www.comusparanormalinvestigations.org/.

23/02/2005

Chapter 4

HIDDEN AMONG THE TREES

THE LOG CABIN IN THE NEXT SERIES OF PHOTO-graphs offers visual proof that quantum energy exists. The cabin itself remains a focal point for the quantum spirits that seem to linger around the building's structure.

Once it became clear that quantum energy had been discovered within the photographs, I founded CPI Investigations to investigate.

The photograph below seems to show a small white circular image that is visible in between the split rail fence. The tiny white figure appears to be hovering just above the broken section of fence. This unearthly creature appears to have a set of horns located on top of its head, and they seem to transform from a white, bone-like color into a darker grayish hue that turns black at the tips.

This being has two small and darkened areas located where the eyes should be. The face is expressionless, and it appears to be formed from solid bone. I refer to this creature as "The Comus Creature."

White circular image of the Comus Creature

This creature in question was photographed hovering between a set of trees. The unearthly chalk-faced creature appeared in the front yard of an abandoned log cabin on a picture-perfect day in the Comus location.

I display this unsettling image of the being with a photograph of another skull, which was allegedly discovered around 1880 in a burial mound in Bradford County, PA, just northwest of Scranton. The Bradford County skull, known as the Skull of Sayre, was unearthed with several other strange skulls, which some would suggest to be from some sort of extraterrestrial colonizing. Although the skeletal remains were anatomically correct as human, the skulls did appear non-human.

The Sayre skull has bony projections located just above each eyebrow ridge, believed to be two-inch horns. The skeleton was giant.

Some believe that the bones may have been buried around 1200 A.D., but no such image has yet been captured that could support the theory of such an otherworldly being existing on the planet, like the Skull of Sayre—at least not until the image of the Comus Creature was captured.

When the Comus Creature figure is compared with the skull from Sayre, PA, the likeness was uncanny. I thought that the creature's head was hovering above the ground when I took the photograph.

After learning about the Horned Skull of Sayre, I reexamined the Comus photograph and realized that the head of the creature might not have been hovering as first thought. The creature may have been standing on the ground as it looked on toward me. When compared to the height of the surrounding trees, it appears that the creature was giant— hovering nearly eight feet tall.

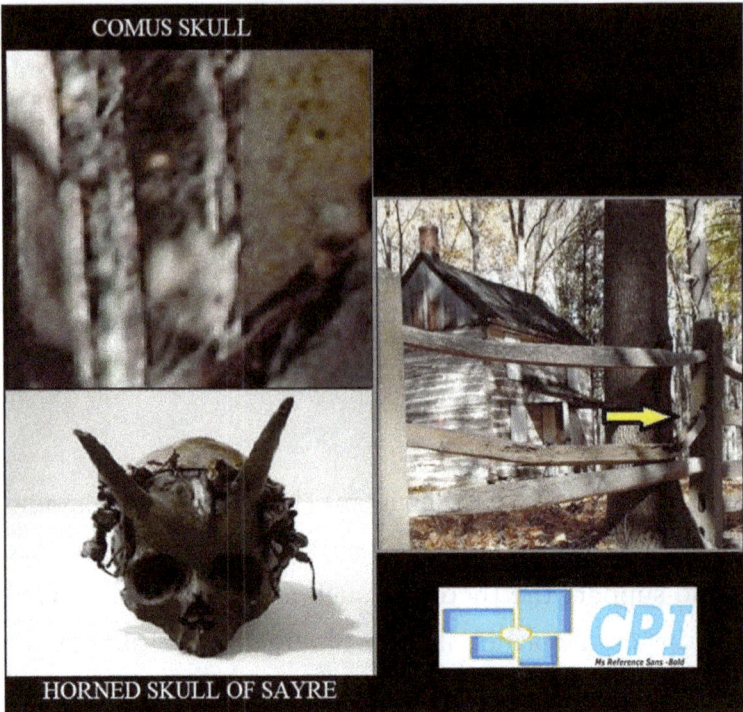

COMUS SKULL

HORNED SKULL OF SAYRE

CPI

Ms Reference Sans -Bold

The Horned Skull and the Comus Apparition

Some Native Americans refer to this creature as nothing more than a "Nature Spirit," which instantly eased my concerns about what I had most likely captured on film.

If the Comus creature is indeed related to the remains found in Bradford County, I considered the next obvious question: "Did these creatures inhabit Earth, and if so, what caused their extinction?" This is one of many questions I am hoping an open-source project of scientific investigators can help to answer. I believe that this is the first time in human history that scientific study can be conducted on images of supernatural beings and is the very reason for establishing the CPI Open-Source Research Project.

Investigators can now compare the Comus Creature image with the Sayre skull image. The Horned Skull of Sayre photograph suggests a being with very large eyes, while the Comus Creature photograph suggests a creature with smaller eyes.

In addition, if one were to draw a straight line from the Comus location site directly north, this imaginary line does intersect with Sayre, PA, where the Horned Skull of Sayre was discovered. When drawn on a map, this line is so exact that simply a slight degree of deviation can be recorded, virtually linking these two sites together in a theoretical Ley line.

I am positive that capturing apparitional images during the light of day at this location in the future is quite possible. Doing so will surely bring an entirely new perception to the realm of paranormal investigation, as it's now possible to conduct these types of investigation during the light of day. This concept will lend itself to capture and analyzing better quality of evidence that is not often witnessed with night time photography. This new and controversial concept is sure to become the next leap into a new study in quantum physics for years to come.

Chapter 5

A CALL TO ARMS

THE NEXT SERIES OF IMAGES HIGHLIGHT AN ARRAY of faces charging the camera. These faces range in size from very small to very large.

One such face captured on film is in the center of the snapshot, and it appears to be wearing some sort of ancient military helmet. It is clear that these spectral images can occupy the same space at the same time by layering themselves on top of one another, making it a bit difficult to see all the images right away. However, with a little patience, the images will become more apparent. Over the years I made several attempts to identify this Greek, mythical-looking helmet, with little success.

A Call to Arms—Original image

Face to Face

The photographs next page are called, "Face-to-Face," showing a solid-looking image of what seems to be the face of an Indian warrior peering around the corner of a tree.

The Indian's head resembles features often seen in African American men. I believe that this type of Indian is described as what many people call a "black Indian" or an "indigenous" person. The word "indigenous" is a term that refers to people of African American heritage who fought

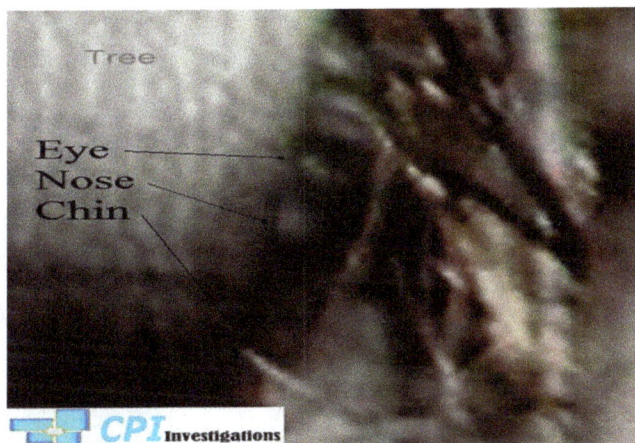

alongside Native Americans throughout the early part of North American history.

In the upcoming image, you may notice that we have taken the liberty to duplicate the right side of the peering chief's face. We joined this together to make his face look whole. This is our attempt to show what the "man" possibly looked like prior to his death. From the original photograph, we did not have enough area of the center section, so we did the best we could to present a full image of how the man once looked.

While preparing this work for publication, we discovered a second person in the Native American figure seen at the side of the tree. In the photograph next to the CPI creation, we circled what we believe are two Native American (Squaw) women side-by-side. We colorized them with red to make them stand out.

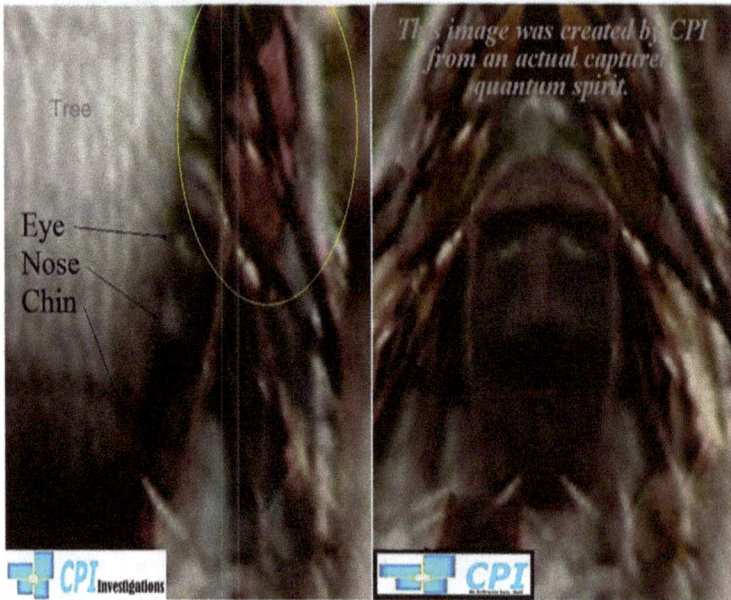

Eye
Nose
Chin
Tree

This image was created by CPI from an actual captured quantum spirit.

Home Sweet Home

The photograph on the next page is entitled, "Home Sweet Home." It shows the log cabin where the apparitions gathered. This was the third photograph I took that day.

None of these faint images seen in this photograph could have ever been captured at night. This supports our claim that investigating quantum energy in nature should be conducted in ideal light conditions and thermal imaging equipment should never be used, as it only robs the spirits of nature's display of beauty.

Note: The date on the camera was incorrect at the time the photo was taken. The actual date was October 22, 2005.

Home Sweet Home

The two photographs on these pages are called, "Whispers in the Woods." These images show a hint of faces to the right side of the cabin. Many faces are seen overlapping one another.

Whispers in the Woods

A forward-looking face appears in the upper left corner and was discovered on the narrow tree seen in the original photograph. Only the left side of the entity's face appears on the tree. CPI decided to place the left side of the entity's face on the left side of the photo to make the face look whole. We only did this in our attempts to identify the person.

Below is a black and white image of a man taken from the bark of a tree.

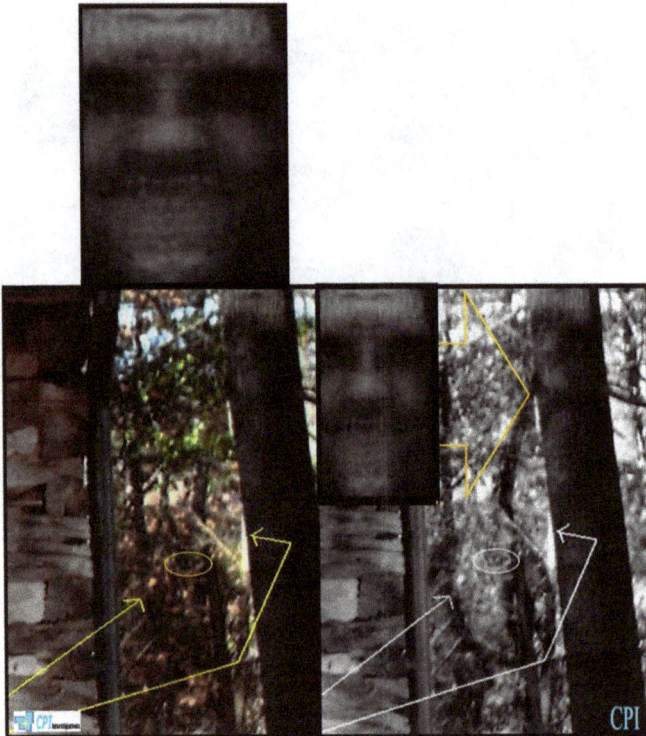

Mirror, Mirror

Next page is "Mirror-Mirror," an image that I believe captured the spirit of Pontiac, a chief of the Ottawa tribe. Above Chief Pontiac's left eye is another spirit, which we believe to be Chief Naiche, one of Geronimo's first lieutenants. He is quite difficult to see; however, you may notice what we at CPI believe to be his left eye. We urge readers to visit the Internet to locate an image of Chief Naiche to compare.

CPI believes that each image bears a striking resemblance to the famed Indian chiefs. Some experts we consulted found it hard to believe that so many historical spirits could be captured at one location, but remember, it's common to socialize with your peers. We do that in our society each day, so why wouldn't quantum spirits?

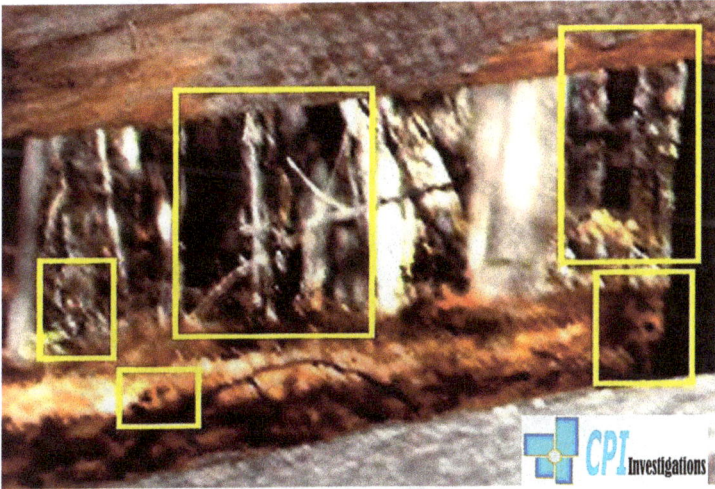

Why it is so hard to believe that social status in the afterlife would be different? Many of the figures discovered in these photographs fought and died together. Many of them probably carried the same values during their earthly existence, and probably continue to hold the same strong beliefs in death.

The Circled Eye of Chief Pontiac

Look at a painting of Chief Pontiac and you would discover that the shapes of our eyes are unique to every one of us. Below I have circled the eye of what we believe is the captured eye and partial face of Chief Pontiac.

CPI discovered that Chief Pontiac had a unique eye shape. There's about nine different eye shapes in the world; starting with Round, Roundish-Almond, Almond, Thin Almond, Droopy Hooded, Hooded and Asian eyes. It appears to CPI that Chief Pontiac's eye shape could have its own category. His eyes were very distinct and uncommon. In this photograph, it appears that our eyes can still interface with the world regardless if we are living or dead.

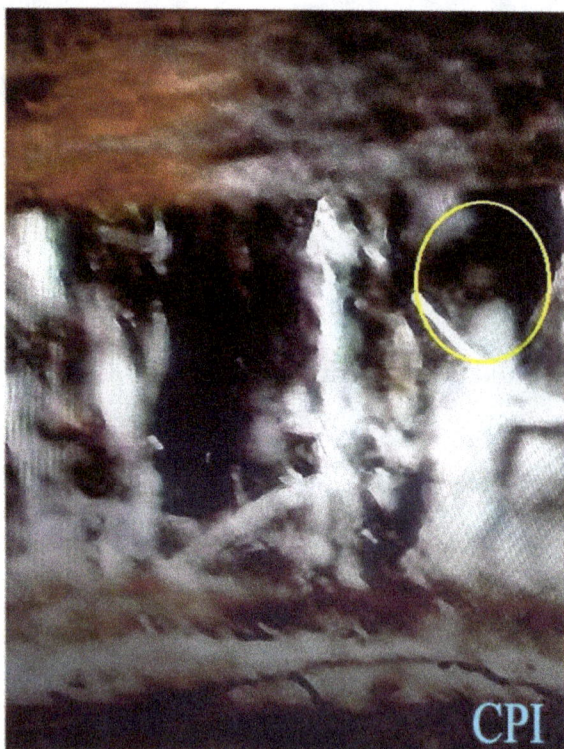

This Old House

This was the second snapshot taken October 22nd. Here, the transparent image behind the cinderblock wall is visible on the left side of the cabin.

At first glance, this image circled in yellow appears to be a pencil outline drawing that was super-imposed into the digital photograph. I assure readers this image is very real and was not placed there by human hands.

23/02/2005
CPI Investigations

Dark Shadows

The next photo shows the outline of spirit formations. I applied color inversion and traced the figures of apparition not seen in the original color photograph, revealing many spirits gathered at the roof line.

In "Dust in the Wind," a tall tree stands to the left of the block wall. Following inside the edge of the tree in front of the log cabin, a face of a young boy peers out from behind the tree. Another interesting image looks remarkably like a wolf or large canine. Near the far-right portion of the photograph, a cinderblock rests on the top row where the block wall meets the edge of the log cabin.

Just above this single cinderblock are two otherworldly images. The first image looks to be a skeletal form, and the other figure, which is to the left and above the skeleton shape, is what I believe to be the spirit of a greyhound. Discovering the image of a dog was not much of a surprise to me once I learned that many tribes revered dogs and often included them in religious ceremonies.

Native Americans believed that dogs helped navigate the soul's journey into the afterlife, and that dogs protected their master's soul even after death. By the look of this photograph, dog lovers have a pretty compelling argument regarding a dog's loyalty and companionship not only in this world but also the next.

Several African American men located within the energy of the spirit seem to also be visible. As stated earlier, it would not be uncommon for slaves, known as "Black Indians," to join forces with Indian tribes to fight the enemy.

This image and all the images seen within the pages of this book can be viewed at:

https://www.comusparanormalinvestigations.org/

The Lookouts

The cropped image seen below came directly from the second photo that was taken on October 22, 2005 and focuses on the lower left-hand corner of the log cabin. The cropped picture that appears on the next page shows a crack in the cabin's foundation.

The picture shows a close-up shot of that crack. There appears to be no less than four separate spirit faces peering out from under the shallow cellar. This photograph gives me the creeps whenever I study it. I shudder to think what it would be like to stay the night in a place like this all alone.

I would like to add that this photo disturbed me quite a bit once I realized that I was clearly the target of interest. Unlike the previous images in the book, this photograph has been color-balanced and slightly enhanced in order to improve the detail of the picture. The shadows and shapes that are seen in the photograph have not been tampered with, and they remain unchanged to this day.

CPI believes that none of these spirits in these three photographs could have been seen with the naked eye. I do not recall the exact time these photographs were taken that morning. However, if you notice the shadows seen across the front door and the lower right boarded up window. This should be a guide for those who are wanting to establish a time frame when the photographs were taken.

Confederate General Albert G. Jenkins

The photographs also captured a few spirits from the Civil War. Below, high in a tree appears to be the captured quantum energy of Confederate General Albert G. Jenkins.

The image next page is the original. Below you will see I have overlaid an image with a photograph of the general that we discovered online. Before discovering the image of the man, none of our staff had ever heard of a general Jenkins, but we searched history books until we came upon Albert Jenkins. When we scanned the last known photograph of Albert into the computer and overlaid it across the quantum figure, the images matched perfectly.

Confederate General Albert G. Jenkins

Born November 10, 1830
Cabell County, Virginia
Died May 21, 1864 (aged 33)
Battle of Cloyd's Mountain

CPI

Overlay Image

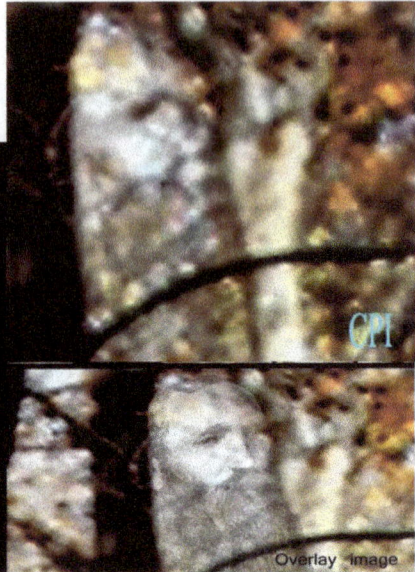

Native American Chief

This next photograph shows a profile image of an Indian chief hovering above the roofline. It took me years until I stumbled upon this transparent side view image. CPI has not determined if the figure seen at the top of the photograph is an actual Chief or not.

We felt that the transparent image seen above the cabin looked remarkably like the black and white image of the Indian chief. Our guess is that others could possibly photograph this chief again located in the exact same spot just above the cabin. Humans are creatures of habit.

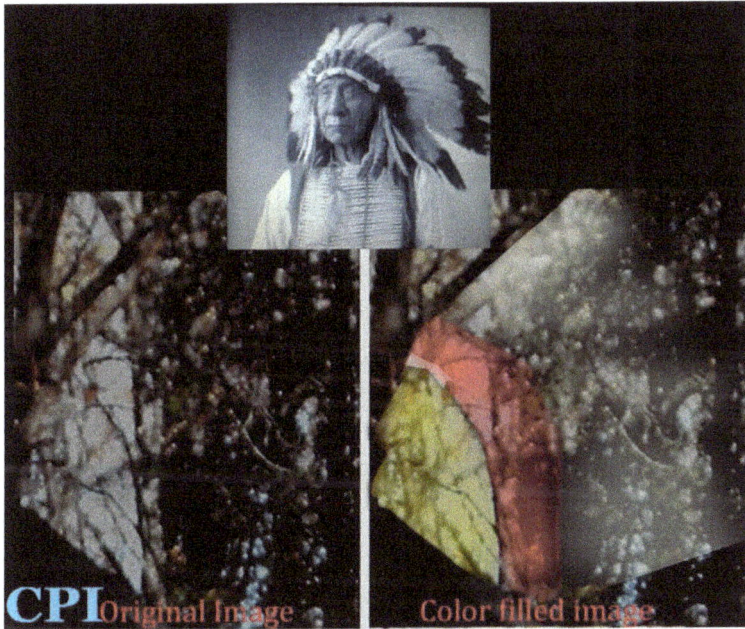

Indian chief original & color filled images together

Native American Chief Location

It's important to be patient with this next photograph; the spirit is blended in well. It was some time before we discovered the Indian seen in the upper left-hand corner of the photograph seen on the next page. He is seen wearing a "High Crown" wool felt hat.

This hat style was widely used by Native Americans from the Northern and Central Plains to the Southwest from the late 1800s into the 1900s. You will see an arrow placed on the following page to help you locate the stern-faced native at the left side of the photograph.

High Crown Wool Felt Hat

Side-by-side high crown wool felt hat images

Golden Retriever

Animals make up a large part of the apparitions. At right is what looks to be the head of a golden Labrador retriever hovering in the trees. The spirit of a golden retriever among spirits did not come as a surprise, as these dogs are routinely employed as sympathy dogs.

There seems to be the quantum energy of a man to the right of the dog. You can barely make out part of his transparent face overlapping the edge of the tree facing the retriever.

Golden retrievers

Man In a Chair

This photograph is a bit creepy for me. I'm not sure why it gives me the creeps over other images found in this book, it just does. In the center of the photograph sits a large African American man wearing a white suit. He is flanked by female spirits. There is one right above the man reaching her arms down across his shoulders. A heavy-set woman on his left wears eye glasses.

Her eyeglasses are indicated in pink and the location of her arm in lime-green. The heavy-set woman has her left arm across the man.

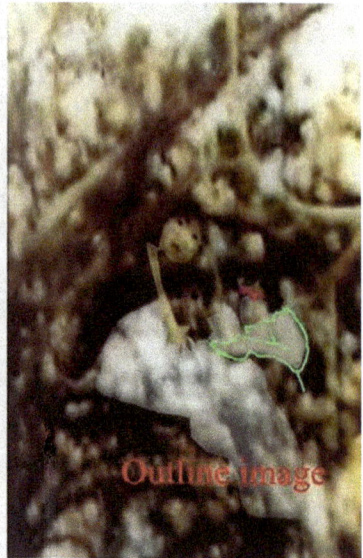

African American man wearing a white suit

Mansi Elder

Below and to the left is an image called "Mansi Elder." Once again, I added a color-filled image to the right. The lower of the two photos show the area where I discovered her in the original shot. All four circled areas below seem to represent images that are often seen in ancient photographs of the Mansi people from Russia Ural Mountains area. It is these images that CPI believes may link the 1959 Dyatlov Pass incident with the Comus attack.

The research that will look into the connection between the two similar incidents are just one of many projects that the CPI open-source research team of investigators will be involved with.

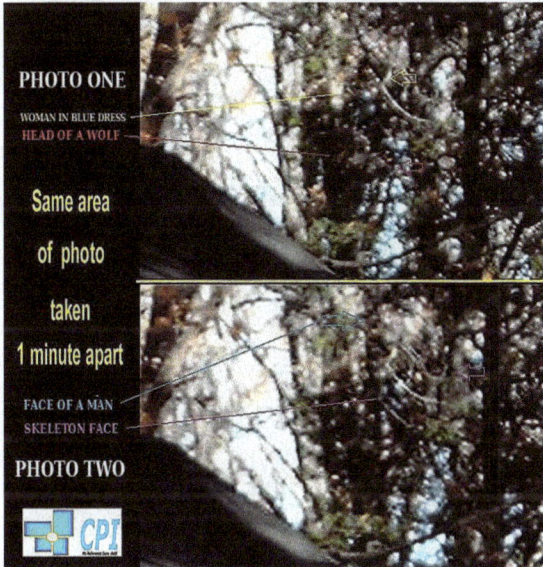

One minute apart

The photograph above shows the same area from two angles. The pictures were taken one minute apart, and illustrate how the scenery changed so quickly. The lady in the blue dress is no longer visible in the second photograph. She has been replaced by a face of a man being crossed by a flying skeleton face.

The Blue Lady & the Wolf

On the next page is a close-up framed image of the blue lady seen here. You can get a better look at what appears to be the side view head of a wolf just below her waist and twice her size. The woman and the wolf are highlighted in the second image.

The Blue Lady & the Wolf

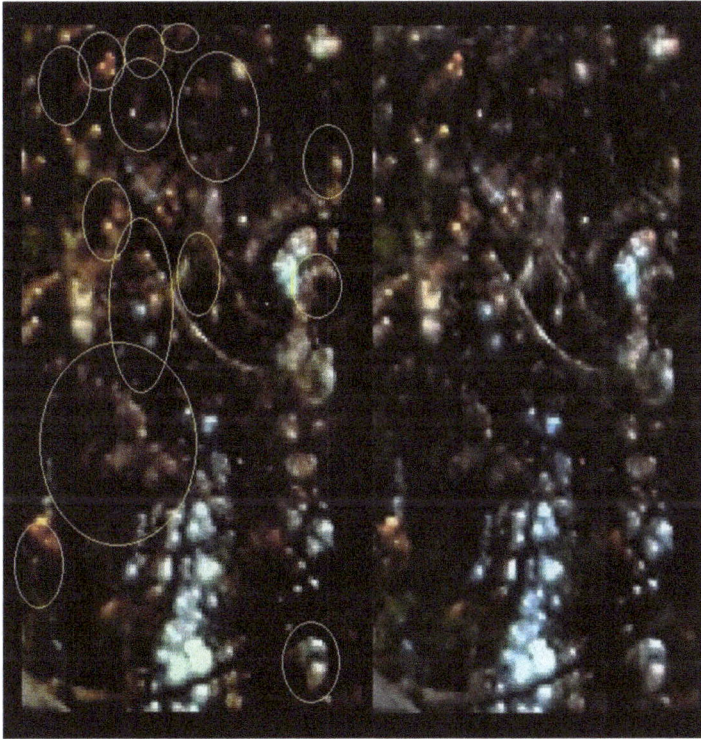

The Blue Lady surrounded by quantum energy.

The photograph at left is a cropped image that shows the location of several quantum spirits that surround The Blue Lady.

Chapter 6

TWO FACES WITHIN ONE MAN

I DISCOVERED THIS LARGE MAN GIVING ME THE evil eye first. It wasn't until much later that I discovered what I call the "Hillbilly," visible in the center photograph blended within another spirit of a man.

I just don't like this image at all. This man looks appalled at my presence. I sketched what the "Hillbilly" looks like to me. Remember, each of us experience supernatural occurrences differently, so if you do not see that exact same images being discussed don't fret.

This photo makes me wonder if I was shoved by more than one spirit that day. The area I have circled on the left shows the face of what I refer to as the "Hillbilly." I created a sketch in the center to help the reader locate this entity.

The photo on the right is showing how the "Hillbilly" spirit is part of a much larger spirit who appears bothered by my presence on the property.

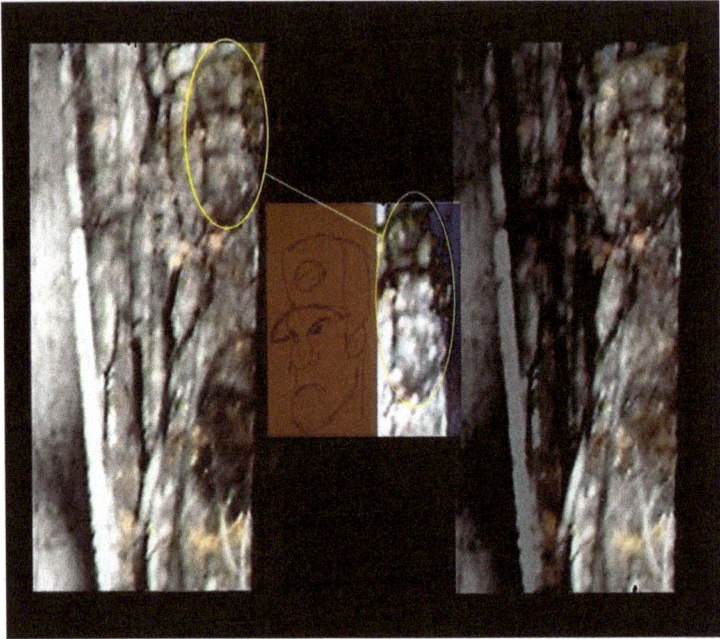

Hillbilly man image

The Three-Headed Dog

For this next photograph, I am looking to the entire CPI investigative community to share their ideas about what this might be. When I first noticed this image of the "creature" located in the upper right picture frame of the photograph window, it appears to be the head of a canine. However, when studying the image over time, it takes on the appearance of a large, partly shadowed face.

The three-headed dog image

Many may see the image of a dog as they view the upper photo pane window. Sometimes, this dog looks as if it's a combination of creatures. What is seen depends on the perspective of the viewer.

For sake of argument, let's say this creature might be some sort of a canine. However, that does not explain the odd-looking legs and paws. These features look otherworldly.

My question is this: if the creatures seen here can be linked to known images historically discussed with regards to the Underworld, could it be possible that this is the mythical creature Cerberus, the three-headed dog that guards the gates to the Underworld?

Regardless of what this creature might have been, just the thought that it could have at any moment rushed at me from the tree-line sends shivers down my spine.

I believed I had discovered all the quantum energy that could be discovered in one section of photographs, but I was wrong. The next viewing of the same photograph revealed more undiscovered images. During years of research into the otherworldly images. I would soon discover that many of the quantum spirits did not appear within human vision. It would be this revelation that would be the ground work to the creation of the Iroquois technology.

During the infancy stages of the Iroquois Technology, I would establish programmable features that allowed me to control tint, brightness, balance, and even texture of the

quantum filled photographs. The application I created had more than a dozen different effects. It wasn't long before I realized that each effect brought forth hidden images that could not be seen with the naked eye. What was revealed did not seem possible. Even though I was dealing with quantum energy, I must say I am still not convinced of what I am about to suggest as authentic.

The next several images appeared within the photographs after applying a textured effect to the image. After witnessing what the textured effect revealed I then returned to the original photograph and could clearly see the hulking spirit.

The outline of a very large Native American could be seen touching the cheek of an infant. To confirm that I was seeing exactly what I thought I was seeing. I placed a piece of tracing paper over the computer screen, taping off only the top corners. I traced the lines that I could see clearly through the paper.

The traced lines displayed an image of an Indian warrior. The size of quantum energy seen in this example might account for the large pounding footsteps I encountered during my face-to-face standoff. While observing the visage of this hulking spirit only helps to recall the words seen in the Bible. ". . . There were giants in the earth in those days."

What follows is the original photograph to compare with my discovery:

Native American man giving comfort tracing paper

Hulking Spirit Showing Love

Confirming whether this is or is not the quantum energy of a Native American man giving comfort to a small child was largely due to the development of Iroquois Technology.

The photograph on the next page is another excellent example of how faces are blended among the trees. This side view image of a bearded man was not discovered until 2012. As with all of the October 22, 2005 photographs, I had no control over the quantum energy and how they were displayed that day. What was captured that day only represents a moment in time.

Although difficult to see, there appears to be the figure of a chubby-cheeked boy in the upper right-hand corner of the original photograph. He looks to be wearing an orange colored t-shirt. I have placed an arrow to indicate his location.

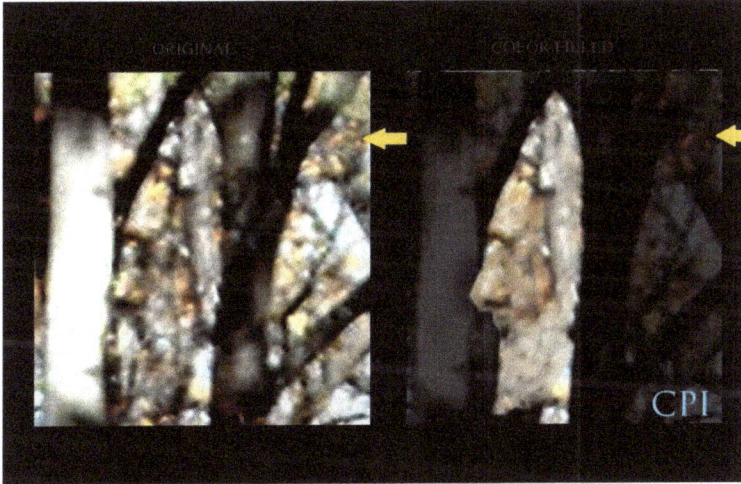

White haired man with beard seen in trees

This next section is one of emotion and honor for me. As stated earlier, when it comes to quantum energy, each person viewing the images seen within these pages may see something a little bit different than the next person. Some may claim that what is visible is not authentic and those who do not see the same exact thing feel it only proves this fact. This only proves that humans are all different.

There is no other uniformed hat that is more recognizable than the traditional firefighter's helmet. When I discovered what looked to me as the quantum energy of a firefighter surrounded by women and children wearing what looked to be a Cairns style New Yorker helmet, it was highly inspiring for me. In the upper right-hand corner of the below photograph I have placed the image of a Cairns black New York leather helmet. If you follow the yellow line down into the top of the circle, there looks to be a firefighter seen huddled together with women and children wearing a similar helmet to the Cairns style.

For me, this photograph suggests that love, life, and laughter do not have to end at the grave, as so many of us have been led to believe. In these photographs, human nature is alive and well. The distinguishing characteristics that make us human are not as superficial as one might think. I see a group of women and children who trust and love each other. Let me tell you one thing, there is not a firefighter out there who wore this style of helmet that could not identify something as important as a leather style helmet. I would know one in this realm and the next!

Chapter 7

MYTHS AND MYSTERIES

I WOULD LIKE TO ATTEMPT TO CLEAR UP A FEW OF the world's unsolved mysteries. The supernatural world often revolves around four basic categories of strange unexplained events.

One is the existence of ghosts. Another is who or what influenced great pyramid structures around the globe. The third is a controversial argument about elusive creatures such as the Loch Ness Monster and Bigfoot. Lastly, I will discuss aliens and UFOs.

After eleven years of research, we at CPI are quite confident that the answer to solving all those seemingly separate mysteries shall come down to one answer, and that answer will one day be "Quantum Energy." This newly discovered energy is most likely responsible for more than 80 percent of the world's unexplained phenomena. In this next section, I will explain how quantum energy is responsible for these inexplicable global phenomena.

When it comes to spirits and the ability to believe in them, we must first answer why it seems that Indians above all others appear to be the most powerful of all quantum energy at haunted locations in nature. How is it possible that one culture of people seems to have cornered the market on power and respect in the afterlife?

Throughout the book, it's easy to see who has the brute force among all the apparitions captured. It's the native spirits who seem to have the ability to reshape their energy by making their heads very large. There are nonnative spirits that appear very large in the photographs as well, but it seems the quantum energy of Indian spirits display a unique ability to enlarge their heads. This appears to be a show of exceptional quantum ability that is not seen with many other spirits seen in the cropped images.

The reason the Indian people may have this advantage over non-Indians is that culturally, Indians have always respected and understood nature. When it came to something simple as receiving corn, the Indians always showed courtesy to the deities of the land. The Indian people felt that living close to nature allowed them to see into the souls of animals such as the beaver, badger, and buffalo.

They truly believed that "no man could ever be closer to God than he who lives in nature." Initially, when it was hot or rainy, early man used trees and caves to protect themselves from the elements.

Later, when they needed to be closer to water and a roaming food source, pyramid or teepee style structures were made. If people wanted to build a massive everlasting structure upon the earth, the pyramid design would be the only style that could last. At the time when most of the pyramids were built, the pyramid style would be the only solid choice.

Its taper formation allowed the weight of each upper stone to be dispersed across several base stones and is the ideal design to prevent crumbling of such a massive structure. Now with the evolution of lightweight materials, modern-man can build enormous sites like the Boeing Everett Factory that is 4.3 million square feet.

Consider that the quantum energy discussed in this book would not be contained by seashore boundaries. Communication amongst spirits and the priests and shamans who commune with them could be another aspect to why similar structures were erected around the globe. CPI considers the building of similar pyramid structures around the globe because of basic human knowledge and ingenuity. Not necessarily quantum communication between the living and the dead, although this topic is likely to be subject to debate.

The Indian people needed to move around with the animals so they wouldn't run out of food. It was vital for them to have housing that could come with them. Teepees were light and easily moved. Although not all Indians lived in teepees, mostly the tribes of the Plains used them.

In comparison to other cultures, Indians continued to commune with nature and the deities that survive in nature. The question that remains is, if spirits are real, how we can determine that fact when handed a photograph proclaiming to be authentic.

The answer to determine if a photo of an apparition is real is simple once you know what to look for and what makes up a full body apparition.

For example, let's take the most popular image of quantum energy that most supernatural enthusiasts have seen or at least heard about:

The Brown Lady of Raynham Hall.

She is called the "Brown Lady" due to the brown brocade dress that the apparition has often been seen wearing while wandering the halls and staircase of Raynham Hall.

The photograph below was published in the British magazine *Country Life* on December 26, 1936. The image reportedly shows a spirit descending a staircase at Raynham Hall.

The incredible image was captured by photographers Captain Provand and his assistant Indre Shira while photographing the historic Raynham Hall for Country Life Magazine in the late afternoon of September 19, 1936.

I hate to break the bad news to the world, but there's a chance that the image of The Brown Lady is not real. Up until now, there has never been another photograph of quantum energy to compare the brown lady image to. The photographers reported seeing the spirit as a "misty form" descending the staircase. Having already completed one exposure and fully prepared for another, the photographers managed to capture this amazing photograph as they watched the energy of the spirit.

Based on CPI research of quantum energy, no such spirit is ever displayed in a semi-transparent mist without being accompanied by human-like features. What CPI believes are non-human like spirits in photograph below shows how a conglomerate of textures is always displayed with quantum spirits. The photographers only seemed to create a Hollywood type of spirit without ever considering the day would come where true comparisons would occur.

The many spirits that CPI considers human spirits look quite human. Nothing indicates that there's anything in between the two that would consider a mist taking on the form of a figure that could be witnessed descending a staircase without human like features being present. Yes, it's true that the camera equipment that the men used that evening was quite capable of capturing quantum energy. The problem now is we have actual images of quantum energy to compare to the Brown Lady photograph and it seems that the captured spirit might be a fake. The large transparent Indian head seen earlier in this book revealed features of commingling spirits within its hulking frame.

There is another important fact about quantum energy we can learn from studying these spirits are made up of other spirits. As you can see below, the brown lady shows no comingling of quantum energy.

Brown Lady photograph is nothing more than a flat image of what CPI believe is an over exposed image of a Virgin Mary statue, convincingly doctored by use of a double exposure technique.

file photo
used by CPI

The photographers probably found a statue in some church and photographed it and successfully blended it.

The Virgin Mary has been sculpted thousands of times, so discovering the actual statue used in the impersonation would be nearly impossible.

Not Considered Spirits of God

The Bible states, "Beloved, do not trust every spirit but test the spirits to see whether they belong to God, because many false prophets have gone out into the world. This is how you can know the Spirit of God; every spirit that acknowledges Jesus Christ come in the flesh belongs to God. . ." (1 John 4:1-2.) God is attempting to clarify here that when you see a spirit and he looks like God as Man is made in the image of God, so that spirit is a Spirit of God. The images below and the ones you will see later, but these spirits below are not considered spirits of God. It's important to know the difference.

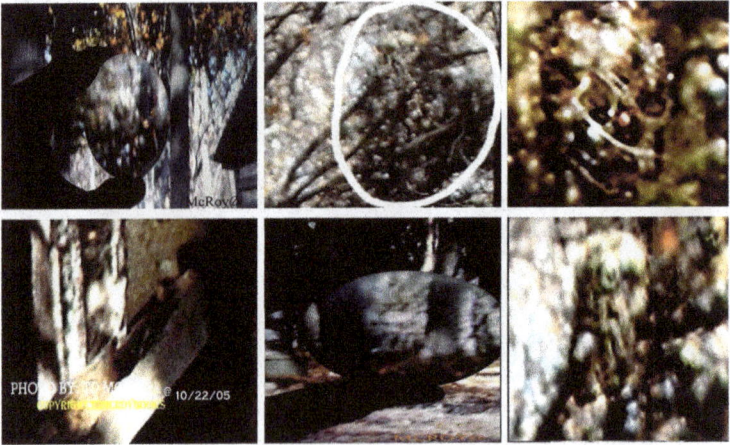

Claw-Like Appendages

The first picture is a 1946 snapshot taken by photographer Giles Healey. The shot was of a mural, which was inside a small Mayan temple near Bonampak, Mexico. The actual mural is believed to have been painted around 800 A.D. The image of the supernatural being was thought to have existed and been seen by the Maya prior to 800 A.D. On this page is the photocopy of the original mural. The painting shows a dancing woman who has large claw-like appendages located at the ends of her arms. It is now my belief that the Mayan were not worshiping these illustrations of these creatures, as much as they were setting up clues for future cultures.

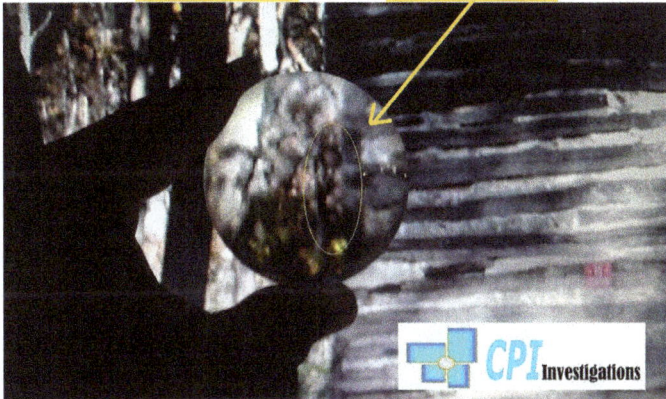

Claw-like arms discovered by Giles Healey

The image above was captured on October 22, 2005. It shows a young girl with large claw-like arms. This photo strongly resembles what the Maya painted on temple walls and what was later discovered by Giles Healey.

On the next page, you can see a magnifying glass is being used to show the girl's location in the photograph.

Mayan Skull

The next photograph shows an imposing Mayan skull. Some say the photo proves that the Maya witnessed the afterlife, which this culture refers to as the underworld. In the background of many of these images, numerous apparitions are visible. However, some images appear to be a bit disturbing, which is evident in the cropped image below. As with the background scene in the skull photo, it looks like a priest is hanging from the tree.

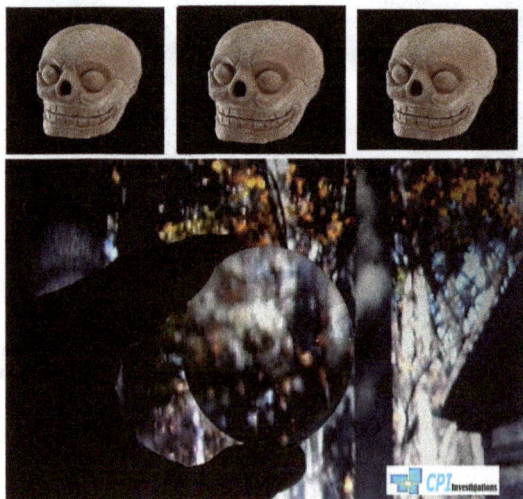

Close up skull image seen through magnifying glass

Quetzalcoatl

The photo below is of the Aztec god Quetzalcoatl, also known as the Feathered Serpent. This god appears on buildings and structures throughout the ancient city of Teotihuacán in Mexico. When the Aztecs rose to power in the fifteenth century, Quetzalcoatl became a hero. Legend states that Quetzalcoatl was to become a priest-like king who was also known as Kukulcan.

What is of most importance is that each statue erected in Quetzalcoatl's likeness has the same spiral-shaped puck located just above the left side of its head.

file photo

The next photograph was captured on October 22, 2005. It seems to strongly resemble the same kind of spiral puck that is displayed on Quetzalcoatl's head. This puck, however, is seen on the top corner of the Mayan sculpture that is displayed on the previous page.

Quetzalcoatl

Below is the photograph of what CPI believes is Quetzalcoatl. It appears with a greenish skull-faced apparition in the upper right-hand corner of the frame.

Close up cropped image of QUETZALCOATL

On the next page is a sketch that shows four 15-foot tall Mayan columns cut from basalt. Each column has been carved into identical shapes of Mayan warriors. Mayan society has reported being visited by creatures that wore strange open-faced helmets that had antennas protruding from the tops of the helmets.

Though the 15-foot columns do not show the antennas reported by the Maya, they reveal an area located on the side of each helmet that may have held basalt strips that at one time resembled antennas.

This area is noticeable just above the perpendicular pieces that cover the ears. With so many of these images appearing to be from the underworld, would it be farfetched for CPI to consider that maybe what the Maya witnessed and sculpted, just might have been the quantum energy of those Titan warriors founds in Greek mythology?

Four 15-foot tall Mayan columns

This next photograph was captured on October 22, 2005. It seems to strongly resemble what the Mayan people have described as "the warriors who visited them."

Note the transparent closeup of a weary-faced man just to the left of the warrior.

The warrior

Next is a close comparison of the three images that were captured on October 22, 2005. I include these close-up snapshots to support the theory that I photographed what I believe to be Mayan spirits of the underworld. Please visit and join the CPI Investigations Open-Source Research Team at https://www.comusparanormalinvestigations.org/

where you can view all the images that appear in this book in sharper full color.

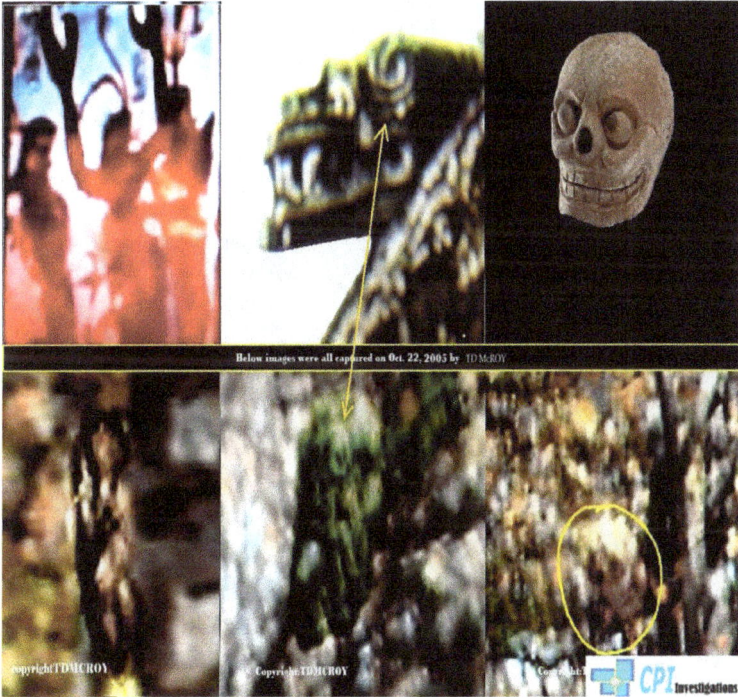

Close comparison of the three images

Below, you will see a side-by-side comparison of a male spirit who was photographed standing in the woods. The original image is transparent. However, a clear outline of the man can be seen. The gentleman appears to be wearing a British general's uniform, and the apparition appeared some 40 feet above the ground. He is towering over the log cabin that is seen in the foreground. Prior to coming to a conclusion as to the identity of this large spirit, I researched every known British general's likeness who wore that style of uniform and who fought on American soil.

To better reveal the outline, the only enhancement that has been done to the following photo, which is seen on the left side of the comparison image, is the blurring of the surrounding area.

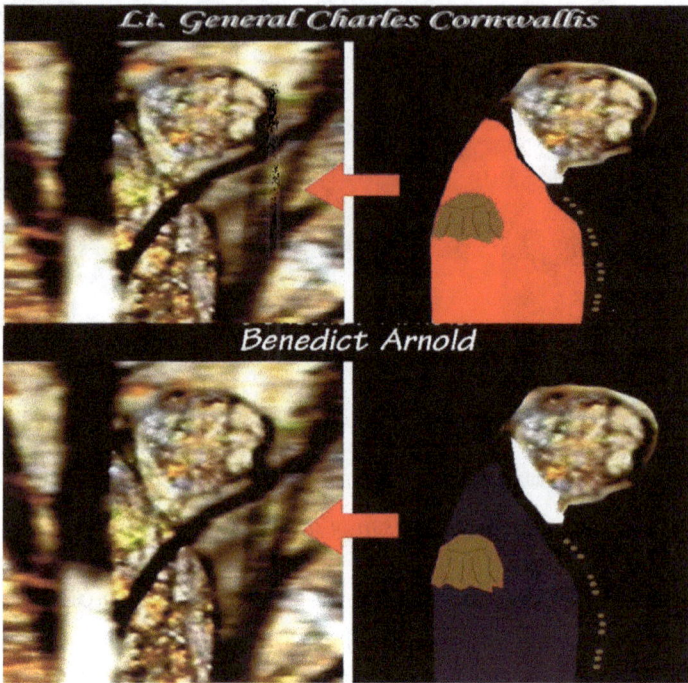

General Charles Cornwallis color-filled image

On October 19, 1781, British General Charles Cornwallis surrendered his army of some 8,000 men to General George Washington at Yorktown, thereby forfeiting any chance of winning the Revolutionary War.

The image on the previous page seems to resemble the general himself.

Before moving from General Cornwallis, I'd like to say we are no longer 100 percent sure that this image on the previous page is that of Cornwallis after all.

file photo

Recently, we came upon the story and images of Benedict Arnold. The image also resembles him as well. I hope readers can appreciate our dilemma. We cannot be certain who is who. What we have learned is that artists of the time depicted their subjects quite favorably; so, with many portraits, those men took on qualities of what was considered "virile" or "masculine" at that time. This resulted in portraits that were flattering, but did not accurately portray what the person actually looked like. In light of that, we have decided to keep the original story as it was recorded. We have also decided to post an image of Benedict Arnold for our readers to debate which man is seen within the 2005 photograph.

On December 14, 1799, at age 67, a true American hero died as a result of a throat-related disease. Records are sketchy about the exact cause of death, but it seems that his death was caused by either strep throat or laryngitis.

In my earlier work into quantum theory, I proposed that at the moment of one's death, the energy of a person transitioning from the world of the living into the world of the dead is instantaneous. This transition saves a type of snapshot of the person's energy, and that energy is what can be seen in the afterlife, and demonstrated in this book.

Theoretically, a person will look exactly as he or she did in life when death occurs. For instance, if someone died of any sort of respiratory disease, that person may appear to be a blue shade, especially around the mouth and nose.

In this next photograph, we believe we have captured the quantum energy of George Washington. However incredible this claim may be, the fact remains that this apparition is the quantum image of someone who probably once lived.

Can it truly be President George Washington? That is a question I am hoping that CPI Investigators can answer once a more detailed review of the original photographs are released to the worldwide CPI membership.

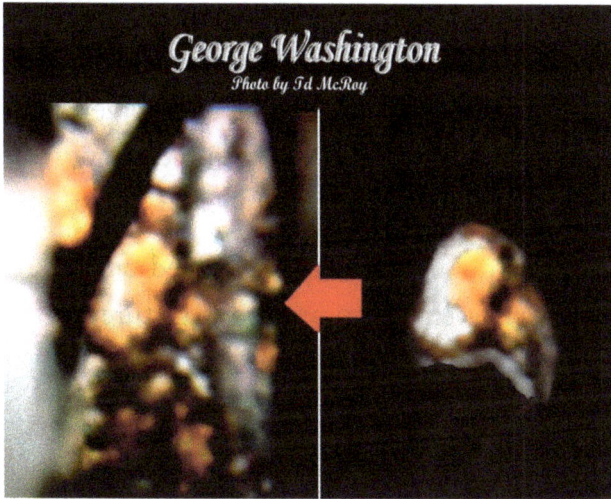

George Washington color-filled image

Below, I have designed a graphic illustration to help the reader better understand why I believe that I captured the quantum energy of George Washington.

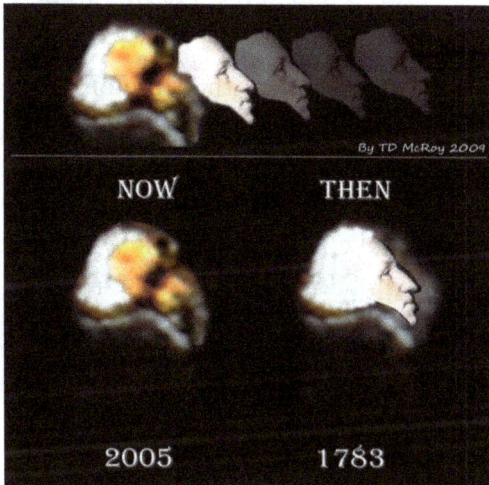

George Washington Then and Now

On the lower half of the illustration is a "Then" and " Now" graphic. The illustration closest to the top of the page shows how I took an actual image of George Washington and then superimposed the photo onto the captured image of George Washington from October 22, 2005.

The only manipulation I performed on the image of George Washington was trimming the picture until it correlated with the size and shape of the photographed apparition.

Once that was done, I used a computerized paint shop program to tilt the historical image of George Washington until the desired perspective was achieved. For display purposes, I also took the liberty to fill in a bit of missing hair on the Now and Then illustrated images.

It is remarkable how nearly perfect the two profile images of the "Now" and "Then" pictures lined up. Clearly, the photograph of Washington in the "Now" image has swollen lips, possibly due to illness at the time of his death. These are the facts of the photographic images that I captured on October 22, 2005.

Note to potential CPI investigators: When studying these historical personalities, never forget the "virile man" aspect. Most of these men were heavy drinkers and did not have porcelain-white skin, as seen in most history books. Keep in mind that the world has many types of noses. Strangely enough, most paintings often show men of the George Washington area displaying very similar-shaped, strong noses.

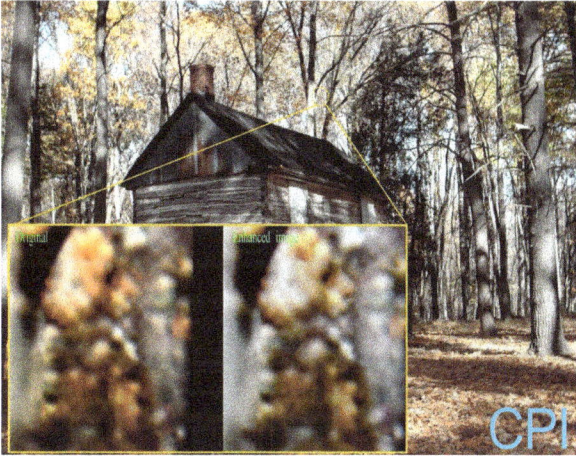

General Charles Cornwallis &
President George Washington location in the trees

The black and white photograph below is one of the last known renderings of George Washington. One part of the black and white painting that seems to be similar to the above cropped images is the hair. Notice the darker areas at the lower ends of his hair just at the nape of his neckline.

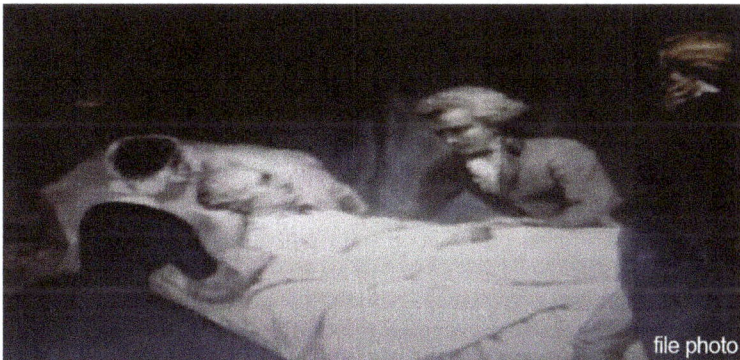

George Washington last known painting in bed

Uniforms

On the following page is another example of how the "Iroquois Technology" was used to reveal images that are difficult if not nearly impossible to see within the original photograph. The cropped image on the left of the page is a color balancing that has been performed to show what looks to be a Union soldier standing beside the quantum image of George Washington. The solider appears to have a rifle over his left shoulder.

The image on the right is the same photograph that's been color-filled by CPI to help the reader locate the soldier within the frame. This image became something of a fascination for my team at CPI. The Union soldier seems to be perfectly aligned with the shoulder of the George Washington figure. However, the head of the soldier seems to be pitched slightly forward as if he is attempting to give the photographer a clear and unobstructed shot of George Washington's profile.

It's almost as if George Washington ordered the soldier to stand between himself and the photographer. Could it be possible that since George Washington died while in bed, his quantum energy is in the parallel universe in his night clothes?

And if so, is George Washington so vain that he is attempting to appear in uniform by having the union soldier pitch his head forward just a bit? Once again human nature is seen within these photographs as the Union soldier's appearance was too transparent in the original photograph to even see the soldier or the uniform.

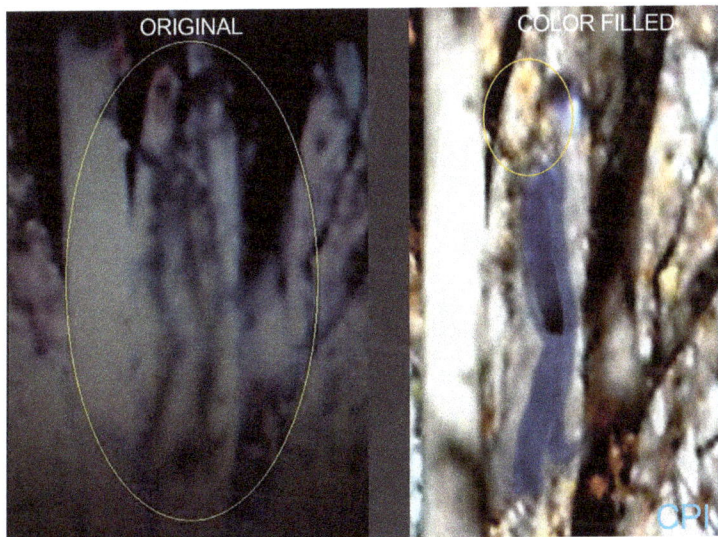

George Washington and the solider

CPI can only wonder what type of tongue lashing the young man may have received from Washington. Remember, not only did George Washington design his own uniforms, he was meticulous about them. Images like these will keep historians guessing what is occurring in them for hundreds of years.

The next series comes directly from one section. This densely populated area high in the trees is filled with quantum energy. You may notice a milky haze that seems to linger in this and many other sections seen in the Comus photographs. CPI has labeled this as "quantum milk."

The original digital photographs have never been tampered with and can be made available for evaluation by joining our Open-Source research team at https://www.comusparanormalinvestigations.org/. However, a few of the images were color intensified to make them more visible.

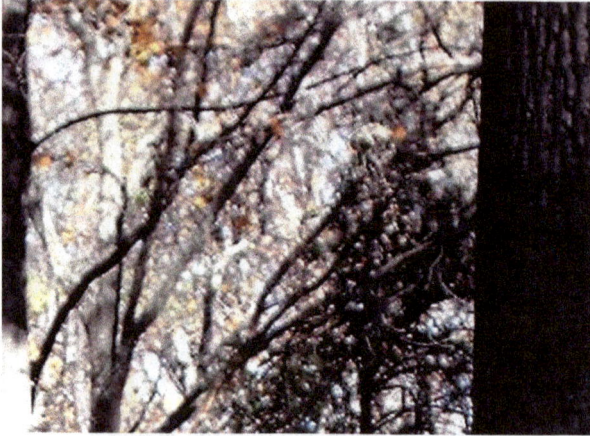

Skeleton Man located light background

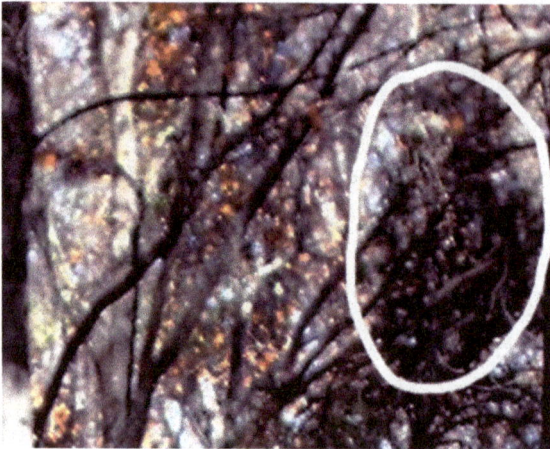

Skeleton Man located natural color

Ghostly conglomerate of quantum energy faces

In the following images, I have added a color filled area where I think the head of the person who belongs to ghostly left hand seen in the previous photograph. I have also circled places where faces of spirits are grouped together. I cannot determine precisely who or what is displayed in this photograph, but I am certain that those trees should have leaves on them.

However, I have yet to see one remnant of a leaf in any of these images. All that seems to be displayed in any section of these photographs are a conglomerate of shapes and images. The lower half of the limb seen in the center of the photograph has been completely absorbed by quantum milk. Visible is only the top portion of the limb. The image in the upper right shows a skeleton man figure within the branches.

87

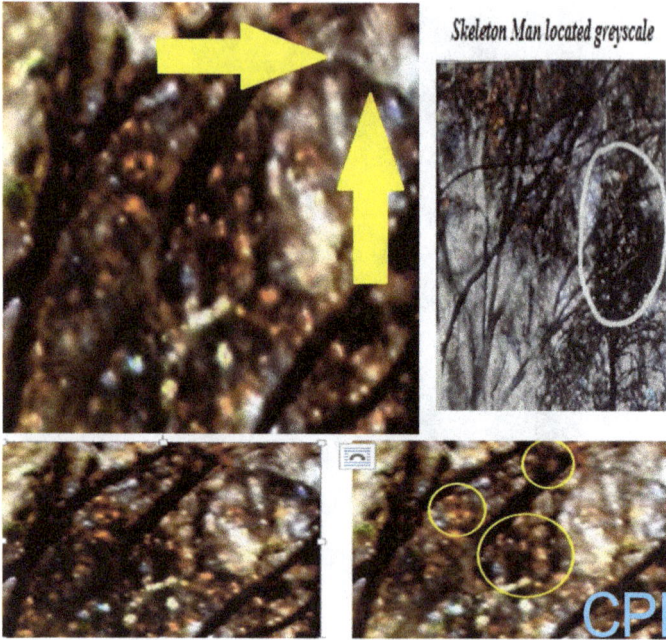

Skeleton Man located greyscale

Ghostly left hand with fingers and thumb

Stand Watie (1806-1871)

A member of the Confederate States Army, Stand Watie was also a leader of the Cherokee Nation. Born in 1806, Stand Watie went by several names before his death in 1871. Standhope Oowatie, Isaac S. Watie, and Degataga, were just a few names he used during the Civil War.

For those finding it difficult to believe what is being presented here, let me just say this: This world has been around for at least 4.54 billion years. Homo sapiens have lived on the planet for 250,000 years. The average male lives 77.9 years, females live about 82 years. Compared to 4.54

Stand Watie (1806-1871)

billion years, wouldn't it seem like it's time for some of the secrets of nature to be revealed? With all the breakthroughs in engineering and technology at our fingertips, we've only been able to explore close to 5 percent of the ocean floor, and that's in our own realm!

file photo

Since the planet has been here 4 billion years, it isn't a surprise that the universe has finally started to give up some of its secrets. Why now, you might ask? In this case, it's because of electronics. Remember, none of what we're examining in this book from the October 22, 2005 incident is visible with the naked eye. It was the digital camera equipment that recorded this quantum energy of evidence.

The physical altercation that I reported was experienced, not recorded. it's important not to draw any final conclusions to what may or may not be factual or possible as it relates to what is seen in these photographs.

Research into these images may take twenty years before we truly understand what's been captured. Patience is imperative.

The next photograph shows a large Native American with braided hair. What appears to be a man can be seen standing on the opposite side of the split-rail fence. I have placed four faint arrows within the photograph. From top to bottom: the first arrow is pointing to the apparition's head, in the same area where you would expect his mouth to be located.

The second arrow points to where the Indian's chest area should be, although it's covered by the fence railing. The third arrow shows where his belly-button should be. And the last arrow should be somewhere about mid-thigh indicating where the ends of his hair braid stops. I did not colorize this entity because of the natural earth-like contrasts

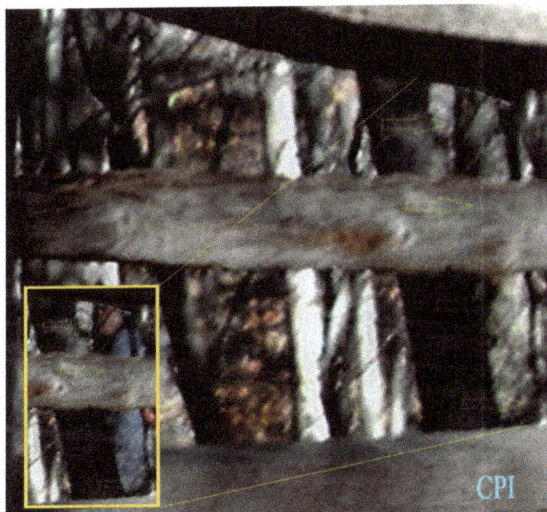

A large braided hair Native American

he displays. Colorizing this Native American would be like placing ketchup on a filet. However, I did decide to place a small colorized image in the bottom left. Just above the tip of the top arrow, in front of the gray faced Native American spirit, is the side view image of a milky-white spirit barely overlapping the edge of the tree. The quantum milk of this spirit is just in front of the braided hair spirit. The face seems to be elderly and white.

This photograph shows the gray face of a young girl in colonial-era dress in the trees watching the photographer intently. This girl can be seen in the first and second original photographs taken on October 22, 2005. In the first photograph, she has her left arm up in front of her face. The girl can be best seen in the center of the yellow square. I did

Original image
of "Sisters"

Sisters enhanced
color image

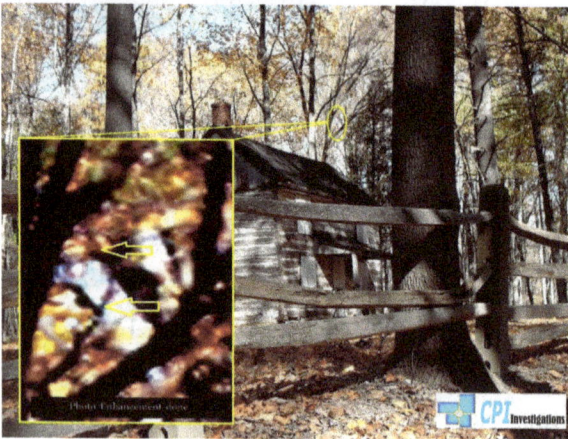

not circle this entity, as with the gray Native American spirit. Adding too much to some photographs can ruin the cinematography of the display.

This next series of photographs depict what looks to be hundreds of quantum spirits. However, CPI is focusing on only two of them. It's what we call "Sisters." Seen in the "V" of the tree looks to be two young girls. One is holding a bald-faced doll in her right hand. We have color filled the image for those who may find the girls difficult to locate.

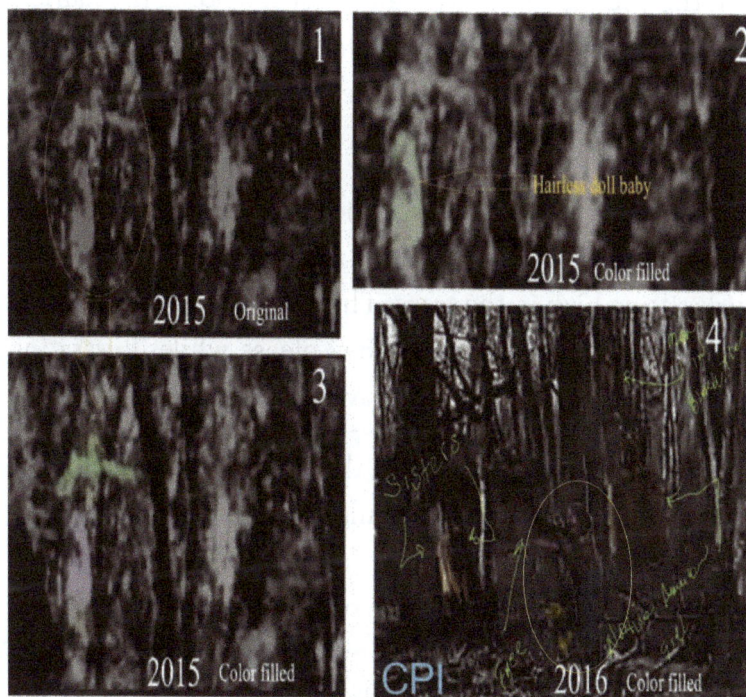

Since the October 22, 2005 incident, the CPI research team has come a long way learning how best to photograph quantum energy. We have been working on specialized camera equipment in the hopes of capturing and viewing spirit energy on a live stream.

We are having great success in this area. One important aspect we always consider is how to make sure we can accomplish the task without disturbing the natural environment. Below are early examples of our technology in action. So far, we have been able to video record the same two "sisters" from the 2005 incident. In figure #2 you can see the younger of the two girls is still holding the hairless doll in her right arm. You also might notice that she turns her head from figure # 2 to the right. In figure # 1 she is looking straight ahead.

In figure # 4 you will see the sisters are on the ground this time. The 2005 and 2015 photographs captured the girls sitting high in the trees. This proves that they are free to roam and play wherever they please while illustrating inseparable bond these girls have for one another.

We find it intriguing that in the 2005, 2015, and the 2016 display of "Sisters" that the younger of the two girls is always next to the taller girl at right (our left). We do not know if this is just a coincidence or provides proof that particle physics is at work here, linking the two sub-atomically. In figure #4, we have also circled what appears to be a young girl facing the sisters with her arms placed upon a fallen tree branch. Although difficult to see, she has a long-haired dog just below her; we color-filled the canine with a hint of yellow and black.

ALL IMAGES ON THIS PAGE WERE TAKEN FROM VIDEO RECORDINGS

Now that we have a good idea of what we could identify as "quantum energy." It's possible that most supernatural mysteries across the globe can be connected to this discovered phenomenon. With this newly discovered information, let's attempt to clear up a few mysteries that have been misidentified for far too long.

Remember, the quantum energy in this book was not discovered in one day. CPI has been studying these photographs for over a decade.

Chapter 8

UFOS AND OTHER
UNIDENTIFIABLE OCCURRENCES

UFO Sightings

ON JUNE 24, 1947, A PILOT NAMED KENNETH Arnold claimed to have seen several unidentified objects flying in the skies near Mt Rainier, Washington. That afternoon, Arnold had been flying on a new course for only two or three minutes when a bright flash reflected into his cockpit. Arnold originally described the objects he saw as being shaped like a pie plate.

What Arnold probably saw that day were the bright flying deities of nature that inhabit this universe. This bright display of energy propelling these spirit entities across the skies explains how separate cultures from around the globe can replicate similar statues, carvings, edifices, and pyramids, as it was nearly impossible for a mortal to make such a journey. However, to subscribe to this theory you must believe in the existence of quantum energy.

It wasn't long before local newspapers picked up on the Arnold story and virtually overnight, increased sightings begin to spring up. These new sightings continued throughout the summer. Many were real but likely the majority were faked.

By July of that year, the public was fascinated with the Kenneth Arnold "flying saucers" story. One such person was a lonely ranch foreman named Mac Brazel who told the sheriff of Chaves County about some strange material he discovered in nearby Foster Ranch. Brazel was sure that this material could have only come from a "flying disk."

Sheriff Wilcox passed this information on to the Roswell Army Air Force base and the base intelligence officer immediately contacted Brazel. By the end of the week, local newspapers printed a story that Roswell AAF had "captured a flying saucer." This story was embellished to the point where people believed that an actual crash scene existed as local artist painted fictional crash scene.

The only thing that took place was the Army Air Force base in Fort Worth examined Mr. Brazel's alleged wreckage and identified it as a high-altitude weather balloon carrying a radar target made of aluminum and balsa wood. An AAF news release correcting the misidentification publicly on July 9, but by then it was too late.

The newspapers of the world wanted to keep the story hot as newspaper sales skyrocketed. There was never, a crashed spaceship, nor was there ever a report of little green men discovered by Mr. Brazel. All those stories came much later with people looking for their 15 minutes of fame and media outlets determined to make a buck.

However, when it comes to the reported incident that started this firestorm of alien tales, what Kenneth Arnold probably witnessed was real, but not a silver flying disk with little green men inside. The photograph below was captured in field where Native American apparitions have been reported by witnesses for hundreds of years. The image clearly depicts the pie pan shape that Arnold reported seeing in the skies.

This image was photographed at night from afar, and it's estimated to be the size of an American made car from the 1970s. This image is what most people claim are daytime UFO sightings. In total darkness, however, the energy glow is all that can be seen.

To understand how the light seen in the photo appears metallic during the day, you first must understand how light travels through air. If air is all the same temperature, light will always travel through it in a straight plain. But with the ball of energy being warmest in the center, the air will be cooler at edge of the energy ball.

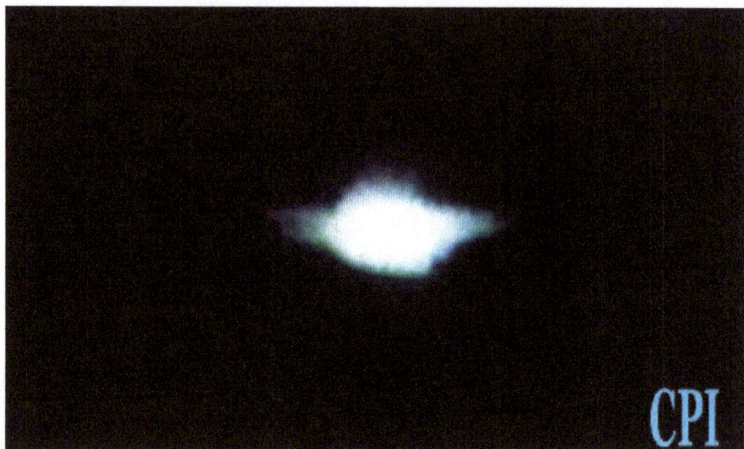

Pie pan shaped UFO

We know this to be true of any source that generates heat. Let's use a camp fire as an example. The further one moves away from the fire, the cooler it becomes at the outer edges. Similarly, as a ball of quantum energy flies across the sky causing the edges to be a slight bit cooler, light will follow the curved path toward the cooler air at the edge. This means that colder air has a higher index of refraction than warm air seen at the center or middle of the energy orb.

As a result, particles of light travel through hot air faster than they can through cold air. When Kenneth Arnold experienced this phenomenon, he likely witnessed a combination of a mirage and quantum energy that materialized into a shape that resembled a flying pie plate.

100

Generally, mirages appear on hot, sunny days. With an assumption of heat forming at the center of quantum energy, it's plausible that near perfect conditions could develop to produce an aerial mirage. Such a phenomenon could still occur even if the same type of an event was witnessed on a cold day. CPI investigators have reviewed more than two hundred and fifty land based and aerial images of quantum energy in nature. In our decade of research, the only objects that could ever be mistaken as UFO can and should be classified as quantum energy.

CPI's official stand on UFOs is they do not exist, nor have they ever existed. The real reason why no one has ever recovered such a craft is because the viewer's brain processes the illusion as a metallic craft when in fact it's quantum energy represented as a ball of light.

However, CPI is open to anyone who can produce close-up footage that is equal in quality to the photos presented in this book. We will be happy to evaluate any images, so long as there is a minimum of twenty images that have never been published. Until that time, we stand firm that what people believe to be UFOs are actually "QEIN."

The next photograph is a painting of George Washington with what looks to be Jacobs ladder coming down from a spaceship. On this next page are images that CPI believes might be significant as it relates to the painting of George Washington.

What seems to be displayed in the October 22, 2005 photograph is a ladder bridge in the trees above where I captured the image of America's first president.

We can now be assured that what is displayed in the background of the painting is not a spaceship as some might suggest. Most likely, it's just another example of quantum energy. Is it possible that George Washington was leaving clues that quantum energy can travel between realms? One may notice that the ladder captured in the 2005 photograph seen high in the tree, is clearly over George Washington's right shoulder.

On the next page is a ladder reference over George Washington's right shoulder. There you will see the relationship between George Washington and a rope bridge forming in the trees. In the painting, the ladder is over his right shoulder-- nearly in the exact same manner as in the October 22, 2005 photograph. CPI has no proof that the 2005 photograph and fresco have any connecting significance; we just thought it was odd.

Ark of the Covenant

During those 3 years of research, if we suspected that the trail was leading us to the Ark of the Covenant, rather than clues to why the supernatural activity is so high in this area, we would had done a better job chronicling our steps that led to our discovery.

Once the clues started coming in, it was like following bread crumbs to the hidden secrets of the world.

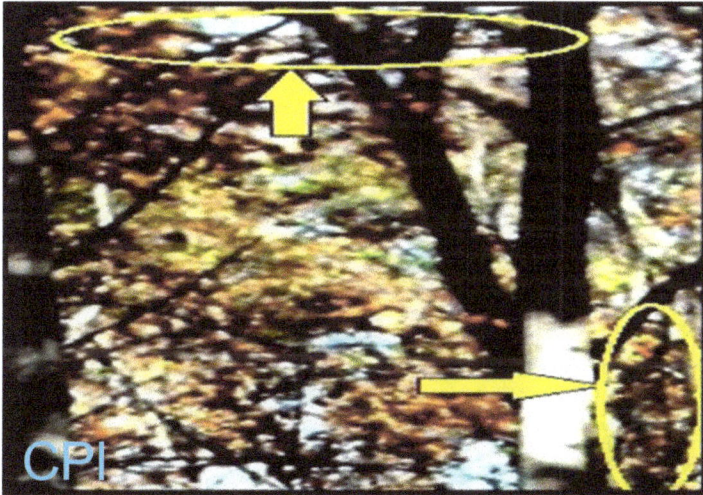

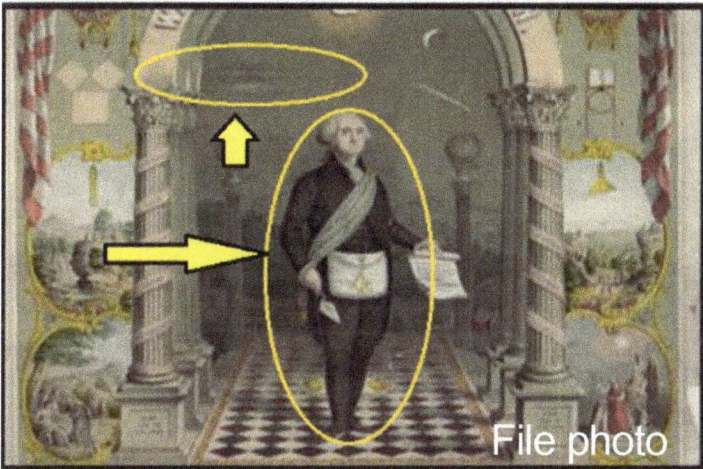

I have spent years combing over these photographs. I am positive that I have yet to discover all the hidden spirits captured within these photographs. As you have seen throughout, I have shown you spirits that tower over the cabin and spirits no larger than a soda bottle.

It appears that many spirits can be smaller than that.

Chapter 9

HOLOGRAPHIC WORLD

ONE OF THE MOST RECOGNIZABLE CREATURES that remains unexplainable is Bigfoot, as seen in the Patterson-Gimlin film. On the next several pages, I have placed cropped images taken directly from the original Patterson Bigfoot film. During my years of research, I concluded that what was captured on film in The Comus location is nothing more than the basic structure of matter.

If my theory is correct, the creature known as Bigfoot is quantum energy, meaning that Bigfoot is a spirit rather than a flesh and bone creature. The body is continually subdividing and altering its shape as it moves. No solid formation of movement could be sustained, as one might see in an Olympic runner. There are unexplainable formations interpreted as small energy releases seen at the surface of the creature.

The texture of the creature should display slight popping and protrusion at the surface. Something should be observed looking to mimic solar flares occurring on the Sun. It didn't take us long before we noticed numerous examples of small energy releases seen throughout the creature's movements.

CPI researchers were sure that the being whose quantum energy was displayed had a bipedal adaptation. To prove this theory as plausible, we knew we needed to discover other spirits existing within the adaptation.

And it was here we discovered that what is displayed is not muscle formation hidden beneath flesh and bone; it was a commingling of quantum energy. Thousands of researchers out there have witnessed this release of energy. What you are seeing in the film is not a creature that is walking and changing its stride. We believe you're looking at a mass of energy that is shifting and relocating within the adaptation. In the photograph at right, the creature's hand is not fully formed. CPI suspects that there is not enough quantum energy within Bigfoot to create a full-bodied display of the creature.

We are left with a creature that can only project the most important features to maintain the illusion as he shuffles off. This creature has clearly created an illusion of extremities not being located where they seem to be located. These photographs are exactly one frame apart. You can see that the creature has not truly moved forward, at least as it relates to his background.

Bigfoot has yet to complete a full stride as it appears he has only moved forward a fraction. Although, it's clear that his buttocks and his lower left leg have lost mass. CPI is confident that this creature is not walking forward in the traditional way despite its apparent solidity. What you are seeing is the relocation of quantum energy from one side of the bipedal adaptation to the other. Having the ability to do so can create the perfect illusion to the human brain that is not supportive of such possibilities.

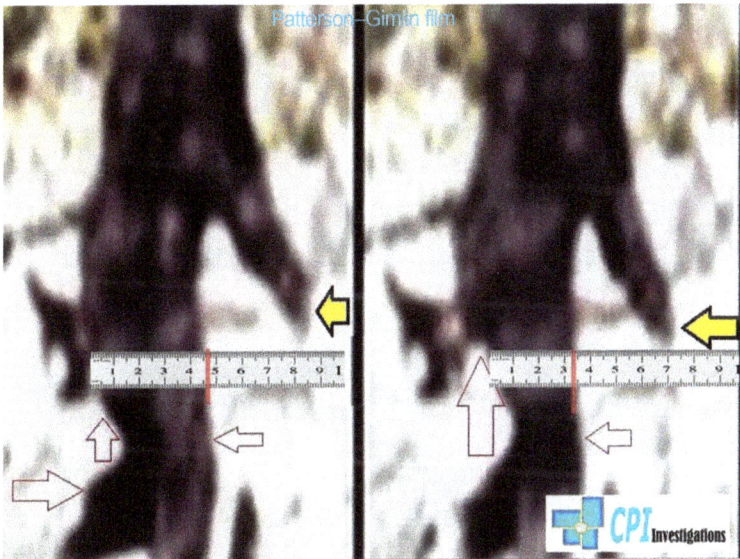

Two side view Images of Bigfoot in inches

Oddly, the size and shape of Bigfoot's buttocks have changed greatly, as if the creature has completely changed his position in one simple stride. Think of the Bigfoot video as something more in line with a college football scoreboard during a half-time show where they display an LCD image of a horse galloping vigorously, just before the words "Charge" appear on the screen.

We all know that there is no actual horse up on the screen. However, if you were to ask anyone seated in the stadium what was the animal seen galloping across the scoreboard during the half-time show. Anyone that was paying close attention would remark, "horse." During the scoreboard effect, we do not pay attention to the lights that are not lit. We only focus on the illuminated display of lights.

Is all this so hard to believe? If humans can create virtual projections on a screen, why can't spirits?

This is another indication to CPI that nature has been displaying knowledge naturally in nature that mankind has only accomplished in only the past 60 years. Heretics believed that there was an invisible world that our eyes could not see. This world was just beyond our mortal vision.

The upcoming photographs show the two faces of Bigfoot. What you are looking at are two separate film frames from the original Patterson footage. The rulers show the changes in size in the hip area from frame to frame.

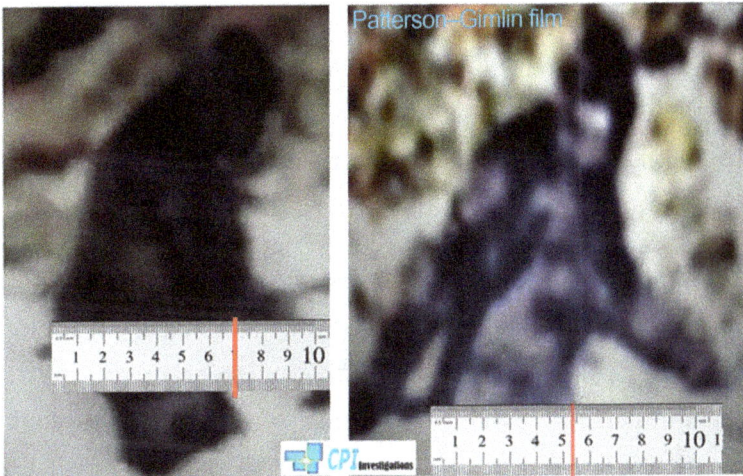

Two faces of Bigfoot

Bigfoot experts refuse to show the public these two frames side-by-side. When looking at the photographs, one would think that they come from two separate creatures. The truth is that they are the same exact creature.

The problem is that the images are seen in the Patterson film and are set only one frame apart. The image on the right is usually what is displayed to the public. The solid black face of the creature seen on the left is never shown publicly, as Bigfoot experts cannot explain the obvious differences. No one has ever been able to explain how this creature can go from looking like the traditional ape on the left to something more of a hybrid-looking ape on the right.

CPI believes that that the reason for the different looking creatures between frames is the result of nature. For example, if you were to ask an elementary school class of students to sketch out an image of an ape. The images of the ape would be similar and each artistic creation would be different than the next. That is a perfect example of human nature and the uniqueness that we display as individuals.

Consider a bunch of spirits attempting to maintain the visage of an ape-like creature as they hurry off. The assignment is clear, but each individual spirit might use its quantum energy to interpret what an ape creature might look like. Each one would be different. This would explain why the sudden change of the creature's facial features because their ability to work together is limited.

Indisputable cropped image to prove my theory

The first frame shows a black ape bone structure, whereas the second image shows a more Caucasoid bone structure. These same comingling of quantum energy can be seen throughout the book. If these photographs displayed in this thesis represent comingling of quantum energies in static form, this would explain why Bigfoot remains so elusive. One thing that I noticed when researching the Comus incident was that wherever there are small spirits seen in the frame, there will almost always be a larger spirit controlling them.

To prove this, I needed to watch the Bigfoot body structure closely for abnormal changes. If I was right, I knew sooner or later the face of whom or what was controlling this creature would reveal him or herself. I was not prepared when I stumbled upon this frame. Initially, this just appeared to be any random Bigfoot image. However, when adding a simple light blue color boarder to the image, something unexpected appeared within the frame:

After discovering the above image in the Bigfoot creature, I decided to create a digital image of what the man might have looked like while he was alive. Below is the digital composite.

WHO IS HE? These beings are purely an optical illusion gifted in the art of camouflage. Study the Bigfoot creature in square inches rather than as whole, you will discover many more faces within the creature. This creature is made up of male and females. We now believed that we were no

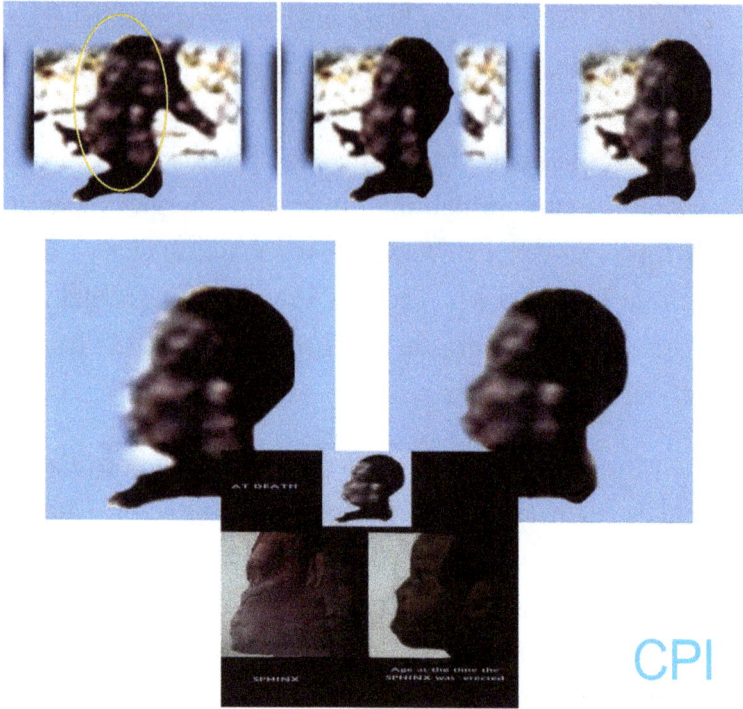

The final face of an unknown man

longer dealing with a flesh and bone creature with actual arms and legs. It was something more in line with a digital display, rather than an actual bipedal creature.

We have no clue of the identity of this man or from which culture he originated. We can only speculate. This is not the first time we have seen "man-animal duality." It's been seen twice before, in Egypt and on the planet Mars. We had no way of identifying this face of the man discovered in the original Patterson-Gimlin footage, but we

112

were dumbfounded once we compared the side view of the Sphinx with the Patterson-Gimlin image.

Three Faces of the Sphinx

We're looking at a Shapeshifter of quantum energy bonding together to complete the perfect illusion of a creature moving across land. The film is not faked nor is it a man in a costume. This creature is purely an optical illusion of nature, able to fool the human eye much in the same way a mirage does naturally. Clearly, this creature is in control of the illusion and can cast any image for human eyes. As humans, it is our responsibility not to take the images presented to us from the quantum world at face value.

CPI investigators are confident that the display of a Bigfoot creature in nature is only used to deter individuals from encroaching upon the land. CPI is convinced that the image of the Bigfoot creature is one that has been used since ancient times to ward off the living. It wouldn't be for several more years after this book was written that the completed Iroquois Technology would reveal an image of a woman in the original Bigfoot Patterson file that would bring the Bigfoot mystery to an end. I refer to it as the "Gypsy woman." You can see the image of her and the use of the Iroquois Technology in use at https://www.comusparanormalinvestigations.org/.

Depending on what one believes, supernatural lore has been fostering the transformative powers of social media, as well as the common, everyday physical realm of modern man in relation to the supernatural, by simply questioning traditional religion.

This seems to relate to the eventuality of mortal death. It should be of no surprise that many find themselves at this point in time, on a sort of spiritual quest. Hence, the fascination with legendary creatures and unsolved mysteries of our universe continue to stimulate the mind.

By now, some of you may be thinking that this revelation of quantum spirits might mean that the world is coming to an end. CPI has no reason to believe such doom and gloom awaits the world as a result of this discovery. You can rest assured that the world is not going anywhere anytime soon.

Instead, try to look at this discovery as an opportunity to reset what we have been told is real.

Dark Matter

The fourth, fifth and sixth sides of existence—Stephen Adler of the Institute for Advanced Study in Princeton, N.J. suggested that measuring the mass between Earth and the moon proved that the mass discovered there was greater than the separate masses measured for both planets. Adler considered this unseen mass as a halo of dark matter. Dark matter has been an interesting debate between scientists on whether it even exists. The reason many think it exists is because there is not enough visible matter in the universe to account for all the gravitational forces that are there. Scientists think there is other "dark matter" that exists but no one has ever seen it.

To add to the hundreds of theories out there about dark matter I want you to consider what I write in the next few pages as a strong possibility to the discovery of its existence. In astrophysics and cosmology, dark matter is matter of unknown composition. This matter does not emit or reflect enough electromagnetic radiation to be observed directly. However, its presence can be inferred from gravitational effects on visible matter.

I believe that the images in this book have captured what scientists consider dark matter. If we look at the basic makeup of our universe, we discover that it is made up of the same basic elements as humans. Based on the quantum energy displayed in this thesis, I can now confidently consider that what has been photographed on October 22, 2005 is probably the world's first glimpse at something that could be considered dark matter.

I would like to further suggest that the essence or soul of mankind is dark matter. And what the images show may someday be the building blocks to prove the existence of this dark force. At CPI, we believe that when life begins, it begins with a spark between a man and a woman. This spark ignites a terrestrial cluster of elements that grows into our earthly bodies.

Just like a star, we are born, and, like a star we will one day die. When a star dies, it becomes a supernova, often creating a black hole. What forms depends on the mass of the star's core during gravitational collapse. We understand that black holes do not have more gravity than the stars that birthed them. On the next several pages CPI attempts to explain what all of this might mean by the introduction of a new term in physics called the Subatomic Googolplex Singularity.

Chapter 10

SUBATOMIC GOOGOLPLEX SINGULARITY

CPI HAS DEVELOPED A THEORY ABOUT WHAT THE soul really is, and we believe that one day the soul will shoot out of our bodies. Once this takes place, our earthly shells will lose the ability to maintain their core stabilization. When this occurs, the human body releases a tremendous amount of energy at the subatomic level in the form of neutrinos.

CPI calls this quantum event subatomic googolplex singularity (SGS). There is only one known example of this type of quantum event ever being documented on a measurable level—the Shroud of Turin. The X-ray radiation seen in the cloth can give understanding to what the Shroud of Turin is attempting to convey. Think of the after effect that is seen within the fibers of the cloth.

The same that is theorized about black holes. When an object falls into a black hole, that information will be imprinted on the exterior of the black hole. In the case of the Shroud of Turin, this same effect worked, but in reverse—God left clues for mankind's understanding. The information from the subatomic googolplex singularity has been left deep within the fibers of the cloth. Much in the same manner information is being printed on the exterior of a black hole.

The quantum energy of the Son of God (SGS) out and the information from the event was absorbed permanently into the Shroud of Turin. CPI wants to make it clear that even though the subatomic googolplex singularity is smaller than any earthly instrument could ever measure. The group is in no way attempting to suggest that the singularity of the event that takes place there could not be extremely powerful.

CPI believes if you could travel far across the cosmos based on the distance of a googolplex, you would become infinitely smaller due to "Spaghettification" until you reached what CPI calls subatomic googolplex singularity value.

CPI is convinced that the starlight which exists within mortal man is equivalent to a googolplex. However, this theory is not based on distance, rather its measured in subatomic size. The term CPI uses for this theory in size is subatomic googolplex singularity. When the subatomic googolplex singularity is reached. The event takes place where inflation pushes out evenly in all directions. This causes electromagnetic radiation at a level that cannot be measured by known instruments.

This massive eruption flings electromagnetic radiation in the pattern of our earthly image into another existence where it gets imprinted. This can account for the image of Jesus seen on the Shroud of Turin. It also lays claim to the quantum spirits of energy seen within the pages of this thesis. At this point, we at CPI are confident that the images observed in the trees are perfect examples of quantum energy. We're sure that the many apparitions there are people who were once of the mortal realm.

We believe that the Shroud of Turin is an example of this transformation into another existence.

CPI now believes there is a link between quantum physics and quantum mechanics, as the understanding of subatomic googolplex singularity should be the first step in understanding the potential connection. This realm has been revealed in this book by the many human and non-human like entities.

These images appear to have left a perfect underexposed image of human features. CPI believes that the features

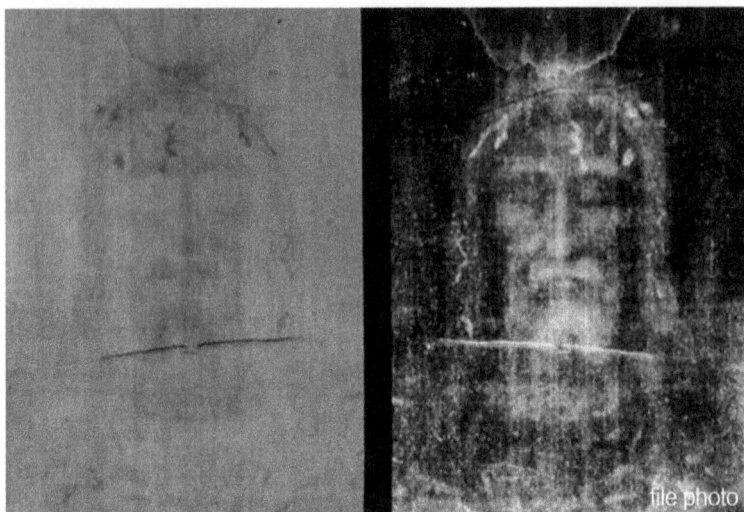

The Shroud of Turin

seen in the photographs of human entities must be how each person appeared right when they died. Based on our knowledge of stars, we have determined that black holes maintain the same gravitational effect as was seen in the star that birthed it.

The images that have been displayed throughout led CPI to consider a theory that the soul of man can experience something similar to a supernova effect within the earthly body at the moment of death. If the starlight of mankind soul can be compressed into a singularity, a subatomic googolplex singularity is possible.

This effect could hurl the soul back into the same parallel universe that birthed it. CPI believes that this transformation from one existence into another accounts for the measurement of dark matter. Mystics call this phenomenon a near-death experience.

The term has provided possible clues that such phenomena exist. The feeling of traveling through a tunnel towards a bright light is a common description of a near-death experience. It's not hard to imagine what type of description one might share if one were to experience a "Subatomic Googolplex Singularity." We can only imagine that near death and SGS accounts would sound similar if one were to survive either one.

CPI believes that once subatomic googolplex singularity effect has started, the person no longer uses mortal vision. This new way of vision can be expected to be more intense and more detailed. The near-death description seems to match the theory of the subatomic googolplex singularity quite impressively. Some may ask, if dark matter exists, could the images seen in these photographs be the cause for what's being measured by scientists? CPI's answer is simple.

If you were to return to the photographs here, one common attribute among the human-like spirits is they appear to be made up of other commingling spirits. However, the sizes of quantum energy seen in the daytime photographs are not necessarily uniform. The images seem to indicate that quantum energy is reliant upon other spirits to exist.

They seem to exist in a realm that resembles a galaxy of stars or a grouping of entangled particles. CPI calls this bonding of atoms seen in the photographs the "Gummy Bear" theory, much like the gummy bears that can be seen housed inside a larger glass gummy bear jar. The Gummy Bears seen inside the jar takes up every portion of the jar.

You can see the head, torso, legs and arms filled with colorful gummies. It appears in the October 22, 2005 photographs that each tiny spirit is only part of a much larger spirit of energy. It seems by the photographs that a larger spirit acts as host for smaller spirits. All the other spirits seen within the host spirit, seems to make up all the other visible portions of the host. CPI believes the reason they comingle in this manner is to reduce particle decay.

Earlier, I suggested that dark matter was most likely these same quantum spirits that our team has been photographing for over a decade. If we are right and dark matter and quantum spirit energy is one in the same. These theories lend support to the Conservation laws when quantum spirits comingle their atomic particles. To do so would make them a more stable force and reduce particle decay significantly; offering a long-lived, radioactive condition.

Science had long determined that there has always been a temporary appearance of measurable energetic particles. This is known as a quantum fluctuation appearing out of empty space. It's now believed that this quantum fluctuation is continuous in this region. As a result, CPI believes that particles of human energy are continual after leaving the earthly body but have only been measured as quantum fluctuations.

What some scientists call particles "popping in and out," CPI believes is something in line with what could be considered a diver entering the water from a high-dive platform. What's being recorded by scientist may not be energy popping in or out. It just might be the aftermath or backsplash of human energy as it exits out of one realm into another.

Where only the splash and wake is left and is recorded as quantum fluctuations, CPI believes that this undocumented parallel exists more a pool of water. No matter where the backsplash takes place, the wake and its intensity can be measured from any location around the pool. Once this transformation has taken place, CPI believes these particles of human existence rejoin their proper place in the expanding universe.

CPI's reasoning for why it is possible to photograph these particles in nature now is because we have reached a pivotal point where the universe has expanded to a point that allows digital equipment to record this phenomenon in abundance.

Think of the expanding universe like this:

If you were to take a photograph of Albert Einstein and shrink it down to the size of a pin head. Then place that image on the balloon at its lowest position. Most anyone who viewed the iconic physicist would find it difficult to recognize the man.

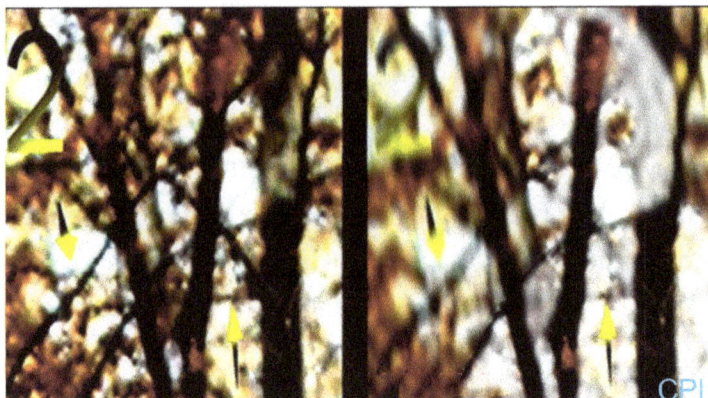

How expanded images work in nature

As the balloon expands, the image of Albert Einstein would become more discernible. When the balloon reached its full capacity, the image would appear larger than the one of Albert Einstein based solely on the placement of the infant on the expanding balloon.

CPI believes this is the answer to why the infant seen in the October 22, 2005 photographs appears larger than many of the adult spirits seen in the trees. This also provides clues that the expanding universe remains consistent, while proving new evidence that the life span of trees can be used as a way to measure this expansion on Earth.

It is the theory of CPI that the gravitational pull of Earth somehow influences the expanding universe. Therefore, the 2005 photographs strongly suggest that if an infant dies, his energy is transformed into the parallel universe measured as dark matter. His energy has rejoined the expanding universe that must exist just inside of our own atmosphere that somehow merges with a parallel universe.

Let's say at the moment the infant died and his soul entered the parallel universe that a tree sapling is born in our own universe. Based on what the photographs in this book suggest, in two hundred years, the quantum energy of the infant and the tree should mature at the same rate.

Actually, only the tree would mature and grow in our universe. The quantum energy of the infant would not grow in the parallel universe—he would continue to expand along with the universe as discussed in the balloon example. Therefore, CPI feels that the rate between both parallels would be the same. One may notice that the quantum energy of the "Sisters" captured in 2005 are quite smaller than the images obtain in 2015 and 2016. It appears in that decade they have expanded when compared to the original discovered image.

Again, this would explain the enormous sizes of infant energies seen in the photographs captured on October 22, 2005. Although the size of the infant being discussed appears to be a quarter of the size of the log cabin, it is CPI's belief that much like a balloon, there is a maximum size that can be reached based on the expanding universe. Quantum spirit energy probably has these same limitations as well.

However, just like a balloon, a reduced size can be established based on desire. This is only a theory, as many of the spirits seen in the photographs appear smaller than an 8-ounce bottle of pop. If we are to consider what these images suggest into the theory of dark matter, we would also need to consider that quantum energy from every animal in the universe that contains the same basic elements of life should also be considered as co-conspirators in this theory.

Canines seem to make up most of the animals discovered thus far. It could be this same grouping of quantum energy that scientists has been measuring as dark matter all along. However, if any of our theory is ever to be considered plausible, scientific research will need to be extensively performed on all of CPI's evidence.

It might help us to better understand why we are made up of hydrogen, oxygen, carbon, helium and nitrogen—the same elements found in starlight. CPI believes that as it relates to particle physics, that a device has yet to be built that can accurately measure what is seen in these photographs. CPI understands that a discovery of any kind is never without controversy. That is just part of human nature.

When the fossilized remains of an early hominid specimen called Ardi were discovered in northeastern Ethiopia, controversial discussion erupted. For those who made the discovery, the feeling must have been indescribable when they learned that the remains were 4.4 million years old. CPI's hope is that someday these images will be considered as important and as controversial as the Ardi find.

While studying the images seem in the trees, CPI investigators discovered something strange about some of the figures seen near the crown of the trees.

Between the leaves there appeared to be a textured formation of color. The colors there did not seem to blend properly with the natural sky. It wasn't long before the members of CPI realized that what they were looking at was quantum energy. The entities were attempting to camouflage themselves as the color of the natural sky.

Not the blue of the sky

For months, we pondered over why the spirits could not create the sky-blue color correctly. Nearly all the camouflage colors displayed by the entities were ideally fabricated as accurate. The greens, the browns, the blacks, and the grays of nature were all near perfectly matched to their natural surroundings. However, there was something bizarrely odd about blue.

It would take CPI investigators nearly two years before discovering the answer to why a near perfect sky-blue color eluded those who attempted to duplicate it. CPI determined that the color of the natural sky is the only color in nature that is not located directly upon planet Earth. These entities cannot accurately assimilate non-pre-determined colors. Molecules in the air scatter blue light from the sun more than they scatter red light.

And as a result, establishing color correctness of the sky has proven challenging. As these spirits attempted to conceal themselves from view, it was the inability to achieve the ever-changing and distant color of the sky that led to one of CPI's most revealing discoveries. We should not be surprised that spirits of quantum energy adapted this ability to successfully camouflage themselves.

There are species that reside in nature that have impressive color-changing abilities as well. Lizards can blend with colors and the textures seen in nature. For human spirits to have this ability is impressive, but not necessarily shocking. Nature is equivalent to the natural world, the physical world, and the material world.

However, nature is imperfect. Not having the ability to replicate the color of the sky correctly has allowed CPI to discover just one more of her hidden secrets mankind was never meant to know.

Chapter 11

INVITATION TO JOIN THE COMMUNITY

Cpi open-source project invites interested researchers to join the research team.

The mission of the CPI Investigations research group is to provide evidence of a midatomic realm for which quality evidence is publicly evaluated. The group encourages inquiries from many scientific disciplines to discuss the otherworldly images and figures captured on film. Rather than the group submitting their evidence to an independent or government entity—which may limit or control the evidence shared with the public—CPI offers their entire research findings to the world, as only the world can truly determine what they want to consider proof of a midatomic world. *100 percent open-source disclosure* is imperative for the success of the project. Supported by the first ever online Open Source paranormal project, CPI provides a worldwide platform for historians, physicists, curators, professors, and students of all ages, along with believers and skeptics of the paranormal to view, analyze, and explore the possibilities of one day proving "The Theory of Everything."

The Open-Source Project is a program that allows any interested person to participate in an open evaluation of evidence. After January 1, 2018, the research group shall go from a private entity to filing for nonprofit educational status. The group was founded on October 22, 2005, and for eleven years operated with an unofficial name. The official name for the organization was not agreed upon until March of 2016 when online members agreed to go public with our eleven years of research.

Currently, CPI researchers only come from the United States. However, we feel by establishing an online open-source project, it will allow CPI to attract some of the best scientific minds from around the world. The open-source concept also allows novice to ghost hunt from the safety of their homes, sure to be a big help to our efforts. CPI encourages all members to share their own discoveries, techniques and rational claims with other members by way of video tutorials. When a member (henceforth called an investigator) discovers a top-quality image appearing to display a clear example of spirit energy, the investigator produces a 15-minute video tutorial. The tutorial must highlight the section of raw footage where the spirit was discovered. This video can be as basic or as elaborate as one wishes to make it.

Membership into CPI is based on a minimum donation. Donations are partly used to develop a membership-secure website for members to download and share their research video tutorials and filters out insincere visitors who have no interest in furthering their knowledge in the field of study. Currently, CPI is not being supported by any institution of higher learning as it relates to the research.

We feel that this type of research is too vital not to be supported and someday governed by an academic institution. We encourage historians to take a leading role in much of our research as we have discovered items that existed during the times of the Mayas, to the kings of Great Britain, and from the bloody battlefields of Gettysburg. As far as we can tell, this existence seems to have absorbed all the runoff from this world like a gutter collecting rain.

Each member will be able to subscribe to the CPI's online Dot TV showcase, where each members' tutorials will be displayed. Our worldwide members learn from one another by producing video tutorials that show from where in the raw film footage they made their discovery and what techniques were used to enhance the final image they wish to share.

The website will not be set up for direct communications between members. One-way video communication (only) by way of video tutorial will be possible. Visit comusparanormalinvestigations.org to learn more.

This is done to maintain the peace between "Believers and Skeptics" and to remind members this is an open research organization to further the study of physics. We only share positive theories here. Members are only allowed to show disapproval by the use of their vote. That's how CPI plans to maintain a worldwide balance of powerful minds all working on the same piece of real estate. Every discovered image of a quantum energy shall be voted on by members. Each voting member shall cast a vote by using their members' number. We call the vote the "YEA" or "NAY" campaign.

Regardless if you are believer or skeptic, each member opinion is treated equally by the power of the vote. After each vote on an image has been casted by the entire CPI group. Regardless of the vote count total, if the vote swayed toward "Yea" or even "Nay," from that moment forward, that is what the CPI official stance shall be.

Each member who discovers a new image of an entity is highly encouraged to display his or her findings in a video tutorial as soon as possible. This shall grant the member an opportunity to name his or her discovery before another member stumbles upon the same image.

All confirmed (Yea votes) discoveries by members will be posted on the CPI public website at which time the member(s) video tutorial with be posted there for others to see.

Time Machine

Our scientific research team is planning to build a mobile Physics Laboratory to further the study into the midatomic world. Using physics and specialized camera equipment, I discovered a way to observe the past. Rather than traveling back to the future, as most would imagine the first time machine could do, the development of such a vehicle would allow us to observe people from the past in real time.

Unlike the fictional DeLorean time machine that Dr. Emmett Brown built in the motion picture *Back to the Future*, the CPI Time Machine will be built on a Peterbilt 389-Glider Kit.

Although the *Back to the Future* time machine had little to no influence on the CPI concept, I noticed a few striking similarities between the Peterbilt and Doc Brown's zany creation. Michael J. Fox, who played the character Marty McFly, drove the DeLorean up to a predetermined speed of 88 miles an hour.

Due to the enormous size of the Peterbilt chassis, at that speed the truck would be a handful to control. Lucky for the CPI group, the truck only needs to maintain a consistent predetermined pace of 35 miles per hour to observe human existence from the past. Doc Brown fashioned his time vessel with a flux capacitor to make the time displacement occur. Instead of a flux capacitor, the CPI group will use specialized camera equipment joined with powerful software to record images in the midatomic world.

During testing of the mobile physic lab's cameras, the researchers captured an image of what looks to be a 15th century Mongolian warrior. The figure can be seen just beyond a split-rail fence, possibly wearing high-plated iron protected boots.

The research group hopes to show that their time machine could likely photograph quantum spirit energy from any period of the known existence.

There are no coils around the body of the truck that will glow blue and white as 35 miles an hour is reached. There is no "flux capacitor" illuminating between the seats of the truck that look like a Tesla coil. Nor should anyone expect to

Time Machine

see two fiery tire tracks left smoldering in a parking lot when research is taking place. The research is expected to reveal (in real time) the answers to what lies just beyond human vision.

The actual name for the concept vehicle is The Mobile Physics Laboratory, nicknamed The Time Machine. The Mobile Physics Lab is a rolling laboratory that allows field researchers to gather enormous amounts of data from ten recessed mounted cameras in the body of the truck.

As the Chief Executive Director of CPI, I want to build the first-ever midatomic research laboratory in the world. I someday hope that most if not, all midatomic research data will originate from the field researchers who operate the Time Machine.

The goal is to continue the advancement in quantum research as it was first discovered. By way of grants and donations through the launch of an Open-Source project, CPI and I hope to develop new interest in science. We hope to establish a solid argument supporting the existence of an invisible world between the atomic world and the subatomic world by the use of a purposely-built vehicle as the Time Machine.

Time Machine

The interior of the lab will be fitted with top quality computers and monitors that shall provide real time analyzing of quantum spirit energy.

It also will provide a room where on location interviews can be conducted. CPI has been working on a somewhat promising theory that suggests high speed, two-hundred mile an hour, end-over-end automotive crashes that appear to occur in slow motion, may someday prove to be the answer to why some people see ghosts. Those are just a few target programs we have planned for the use of such a vehicle.

The Mobile Physics Laboratory is for CPI Investigators only. If you wish to take part in our field research, you must be an active member during our membership lottery drawing. The lottery is drawn on a first-come, first-serve basis.

The earlier you sign up, the better chance you have to be part of the first researchers in the new Lab. The Mobile Physics Lab (MPL) will be constructed to be Handicap Accessible. As long as you can navigate your wheelchair within the MPL without assistance, you can participate. For more information on how to take part in our field research, visit https://www.comusparanormalinvestigations.org/.

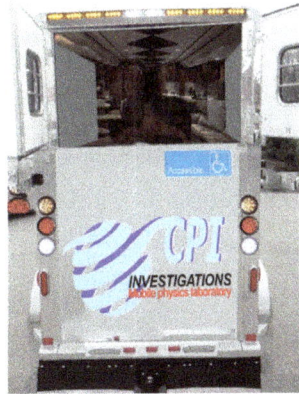

Conclusion: A Poem

If you think about the earth, nature was the first to form. Way before man and way before animals of any kind; there was nature. Trees, CPI consider them the matriarch of existence. They have long life. They have lived and breathe the oxygen of the world from the beginning of time and beyond. They see all. They are the mothers of life itself as their roots run deep into the soul of the earth. Trees are the keeper of all Gods' earthly secrets.

They are the guardians of truth, wisdom and prosperity that await mankind. Every now and again if you watch trees closely, you can see their branches bend in anger as if there is a strong breeze; although there is none. When mankind and his earthly structures have long perished from the earth, trees will be what will continue to watch over the land. The Native Americans considered God the father and the earth their mother, hence the term "Mother Earth."

As they were sure that she was a living breathing energy of all things spiritual and wise. She is the mother of all-things. She remembers every detail. She remembers every child that was birthed from her womb. She is a mother of defining traits. Her love is unconditional. Even though her children have hurt her, she is still mother, and mother always forgives with no regrets. She is always there to provide emotional support when her child is sad and stands alone.

She provides that needed gentle breeze that pushes away those tears. She will always be the mother of all things, which is happiness, and that is love, and she is, and always will be the nature of us. Inspired by the writings of Hermann Hesse.